A HANDBOOK
FOR
TEACHERS
OF
AFRICAN AMERICAN
CHILDREN

Baruti K. Kafele

BARUTI PUBLISHING
Jersey City, New Jersey

For information regarding lectures, workshops, seminars, assemblies or ordering publications and tapes by the author, please call or write to:

Baruti K. Kafele
P.O. Box 4088
Jersey City, NJ   07304
email: bkafele@earthlink.net
(201) 433-0622

First Edition - First Printing

Cover Design
Susan Miller

Library of Congress Control Number: 2004092160
ISBN: 0-9629369-4-4
Copyright © 2004 by Baruti K. Kafele

DEDICATION

This book is dedicated to all of the many teachers of African American children, for the responsibility of educating African American children rests squarely on your shoulders.

ACKNOWLEDGEMENTS

Thank you to my students and staff at Sojourner Truth Middle School and Patrick F. Healy Middle School, both in East Orange, NJ, and Hubbard Middle School in Plainfield, NJ. I've grown so much as an educator as a result of our relationship.

Thank you to all who have believed in me and stuck by me throughout my career as a teacher and principal. I also thank those who have opposed me philosophically. It is conflict which causes a man to grow. If we all agree with one another, growth will never occur.

Thank you to all who were influential in my principalship appointments. Your influence demonstrated your faith in my ability to lead.

Thank you to Kevin Booker, Marva Fuller and Vincent Stallings. What a blessing to have Assistant Principals of your caliber.

Thank you to Sancha Gray, Purvi Patel, Marcia Phillips, Daniela Small-Bailey, Deitria Smith and Judith Stoddart for "making the switch." All principals should be so fortunate.

Thank you to Roberta Leveson, Lillian Hammond and Shirlene Beamon. I could always count on you to elevate my self-esteem.

Thank you to Rev. Edward Satterfield and Rev. Richard Draughn for always giving me "props" during Sunday services. You may never know the depth of the impact you made on my confidence to continue to meet the challenges I am regularly confronted with.

To my extended family, thank you for always being supportive of everything I do. You are a true source of inspiration and encouragement.

To my wife, Kimberley Kafele, thank you for being a "super wife." I have grown so much as a man because of you and our relationship. I love you to no end.

To my children - Baruti, Jabari and Kibriya, I can only pray that my accomplishments will serve as a source of inspiration and encouragement towards your own growth and development.

To my mother, Delores Cushnie, what can I say? Thank you for your molding and shaping. Without you, this book would not have even been a thought. Thank you for being you.

To my father, Norman (Jamal) Hopkins, without you, there is no me. Thank you for being you.

A special thank you to Les Carter who I overlooked in my first book. You helped to lay the initial foundation for my African-centered consciousness.

TABLE OF CONTENTS

PREFACE

As an educator of African American children in urban public schools, the number one crisis in urban education for me unquestionably is the widespread underachievement of African American children; particularly at the middle and high school levels. Although this is not a new crisis, its intensity has increased so dramatically that it appears that there is no end in sight. Many continue to make attempts at addressing this crisis through writings, conferences and professional development for educators but the underachievement of African American children continues to persist throughout the U.S.

When one analyzes state and national achievement data by ethnic group categories, it becomes more than apparent that this is a national crisis with no one region or state being exempt. One could therefore make the argument that the teachers of African American children require a fundamentally different paradigm. In other words, there is either something that we as educators are doing drastically wrong or there is something significant that is missing from our teaching repertoires.

My motivation for writing *A Handbook for Teachers of African American Children* is to offer teachers alternatives to those practices which have proven to be ineffective towards raising the achievement levels of African American children. It is a guide comprised of strategies based upon my years of experience, success and research as an educator of African American children. It is by no means meant to be a "scholarly" work. It is meant to be a "practical" handbook that provides the reader with solutions for a problem that has reached epidemic proportions.

I formally entered the teaching profession as an alternate route teacher in September, 1992. My only previous experience was as a substitute teacher for one year in Brooklyn, NY and one year in East Orange, NJ. My formal teacher training was literally on the job. This required me to learn and develop my craft rather quickly, while simultaneously experimenting with a variety of strategies and practices in order for me to effectively motivate, educate and empower my students. By the end of the 1995-96 school year, which was four years later, I was selected as the school, district and county Teacher of the Year. In other words, I learned how to be effective in a very short period of time and my students benefited immensely from what I had to offer which included them consistently scoring high on standardized assessments.

A Handbook for Teachers of African American Children is comprised of all of the strategies I utilized and practices I engaged in during the years that I spent in the classroom prior to becoming an administrator. I am certain that with earnest implementation by all teachers who read this book, considerable improvement in student motivation, achievement and behavior will occur. The key words are "earnest implementation."

During and after reading this book, you will probably conclude that the strategies offered actually apply to teachers of all children; not just teachers of African American children. While I would agree, I made the decision to target the teachers of African American children out of my desperation to capture their attention. My focus is on them because as stated above, the achievement levels of African American children as a whole is a national crisis.

INTRODUCTION

On a recent return flight from Los Angeles to New Jersey, I was deeply engrossed in thought about the role of the classroom teacher relative to student achievement. More specifically, I was deeply engrossed in thought about the role of the classroom teacher relative to African American student achievement because it seems that the achievement gap between African American and white students continues to grow wider. As an educator, I am clear on the responsibility of the teacher relative to student achievement. My contention then is that while the children are in the classroom, the number one determinant relative to their success or failure is the classroom teacher. It is then imperative that the teacher is equipped with all the requisite tools for increasing the probability for student achievement and success to occur.

Throughout my practice as an educator, I have worked in urban public schools as a teacher, assistant principal, principal and consultant. The student populations I have serviced have been predominantly African American residing in urban communities. This engenders a whole host of challenges that are uniquely peculiar to the African American community which may not even exist in non African American communities.

When one examines the achievement gap between African American and white students closely, one discovers a frightening reality - that as students advance from the elementary level to the middle school level, the achievement gap becomes wider, which implies for me that the longer students are in school, the less motivated they become. Moreover, as students advance from the middle school level to the high school level, the reality of the African American student drop out rate becomes an issue. In far too many cities, the drop out rate exceeds fifty percent of the total African American student body. This is a crisis that requires immediate solutions.

As my flight continued, I pondered over what it would require for teachers of African American children to keep their students motivated while effectively meeting their students' learning needs and therefore significantly closing the achievement gap. In other words, I thought about what characteristics teachers must possess and what practices teachers must engage in for them to effectively motivate and educate African American children. As a principal, I also pondered over everything I would typically expect of classroom teachers of African American children in order for them to substantially raise the achievement levels of all of their students. I then took out a notebook and began to brainstorm based on my own past research, experiences and successes of what works best towards meeting the needs of African American students. The next thing I knew, I had a rather extensive list of characteristics, practices and expectations written. Once I got home, I reexamined the list and over a period of several weeks, consolidated much of it to ultimately form the basis of this book.

As I continued to study, examine and discuss this list with other educators, it became more and more apparent to me that the master teachers of the world probably possess these characteristics, engage in these practices and meet these expectations in their regular practice of teaching, either consciously or subconsciously on a regular and ongoing basis. This is why they are in part the master teachers that they are. The problem is that most teachers are not master teachers. In other words, being considered a master teacher implies reaching a level of expertise in the practice of teaching. Most people however, are not experts at what they do. They may be very good at what they do while striving to reach a level of expertise but in the interim, they are not experts. In the teaching profession, one may be striving to become a master teacher, but has not yet attained this level of expertise. The problem for educators however is that students require that all of their teachers enter the classroom as master teachers from the outset. They cannot afford to wait for their teachers to develop over a period of time. They need their teachers to demonstrate mastery now; particularly African-American students enrolled in urban public schools where again, achievement levels lag far behind their white counterparts.

When one examines standardized assessment data of African American students; particularly at the middle and high school levels, one wonders if this problem will ever be resolved. School districts collectively spend millions of dollars on reading and math programs with the hope that proper implementation will yield improvements in student achievement. In other words, school districts are operating under the implied premise that if they implement a superior reading program or a superior math program, the achievement gap will close over a period of time. My contention however is that reading and math deficiencies are not even the problem. Deficiencies in reading and math are the results of a much larger societal problem which I will address in Chapter One - The Missing Component. For now, if African American children are going to be successful in the classroom and beyond, they must have teachers who possess all of the requisite tools to forge meaningful connections with them. Their teachers must then have the ability to effectively lay a solid foundation for learning to occur if learning is in fact going to take place.

In writing this book, it is my hope and desire that its utilization and implementation will be contributory towards meeting the educational needs of African American children. If only one teacher and therefore only one African American student benefits from this book, I can say that my writing was not in vain.

Following is the list of characteristics, practices and expectations I developed which I refer to now as *"Baruti's 50 'I's' for Effective Teaching."* In addition to reading and studying this book, I recommend that you review this list regularly while infusing as much of it as possible into your regular practice of teaching.

Baruti's 50 I's for Effective Teaching

1. I am knowledgeable of and have an appreciation and respect for the history and culture of my students.
2. I utilize an African-centered approach to my instruction.
3. I have a definite purpose for teaching.
4. I treat teaching not as a job, profession or career but as a mission.
5. I have a vision for what I expect my students to achieve.
6. I see myself as the number one determinant as to the success or failure of my students.
7. I see myself as a role model and therefore always conduct myself as a professional.
8. I conduct daily self-reflections and self-assessments.
9. I strive to motivate, educate and empower my students daily.
10. I have high expectations and standards for all of my students and believe that they will reach them.
11. I instill in my students a sense of purpose for their education daily.
12. I hold my students accountable for setting academic goals and developing strategies for achieving them.
13. I consistently teach with energy, enthusiasm, passion and optimism.
14. I have an unequivocal commitment to my students' academic growth and development.
15. I am an expert in the content area(s) I teach.
16. I utilize a student-centered approach to instruction.
17. I differentiate my instruction based upon the different learning styles and ability levels of my students.
18. I utilize a variety of instructional approaches for the benefit of my students.
19. I utilize an interdisciplinary approach to instruction.
20. I incorporate technology into my instruction regularly.
21. I am knowledgeable of brain theory and how the brain processes information.
22. I am knowledgeable of child development theory.
23. I plan systematically for each day, week, month and school year.

24. I utilize achievement data to develop my lessons regularly.
25. I am consistently highly organized.
26. I have a classroom environment that is conducive to learning.
27. I am a superb classroom manager.
28. I have a love, appreciation and respect for my students.
29. I have an appreciation and respect for the community in which my students reside.
30. I do not fear my students, their parents, nor the community in which they reside.
31. I treat all of my students equally and fairly.
32. I know all of my students beyond the academic side.
33. I attend student functions beyond the ones I organize.
34. I eat lunch with my students.
35. I teach students - not subjects.
36. I make learning fun, stimulating and engaging.
37. I teach and encourage critical thinking regularly.
38. I refuse to accept failure or to allow failure to occur in my classroom.
39. I refuse to make excuses for any failure my students may experience.
40. I accept responsibility and accountability for student success and failure.
41. I do not use the race or socioeconomic status of my students as an excuse.
42. I am a life-long learner while always striving to become a better teacher.
43. I participate in ongoing professional development.
44. I have a collegial relationship with my colleagues.
45. I accept constructive feedback from my colleagues and administrators.
46. I act upon suggestions from my colleagues and administrators for improvement.
47. I see myself as an integral part of a team; not an island by myself.
48. I maximize parental involvement through developing strong bonds with all of my parents.
49. I notify parents for both problems and successes.
50. I visit the homes of my students.

I. THE MISSING COMPONENT

Twenty years ago while working on my Bachelor of Science degree, I came across the book, *The Autobiography of Malcolm X*. Outside of name recall, I had no real prior knowledge or understanding of Malcolm's work or contribution to society. For whatever reason, I read this book with great interest from cover to cover, day in and day out. I literally couldn't put this book down. Even during times when I wasn't reading it, I was processing in my mind aspects of what I read. Once I completed the book, I no longer viewed life as I had previously. In other words, Malcolm's life in print made such a profound impact on my thinking that I almost instantaneously became a changed person. I now felt that I had a job to do and a role to play in this ongoing struggle for African American justice and equality which prior to reading the book, I had no real identification with.

I soon after read all the books I could get my hands on regarding Malcolm's life. While studying Malcolm's life, I developed a curiosity about some of the literature that he had read that opened his own eyes while he was incarcerated. For example, while incarcerated, Malcolm studied and learned about African and African American history. His studying of the people of Africa during both the pre-colonial and colonial eras broadened his understanding of not only Africa and its people, but more importantly, it broadened his understanding of himself as a descendant of Africa.

I in turn developed an insatiable thirst for the same knowledge that Malcolm had acquired. I began to frequent African American bookstores in the New York - New

Jersey area regularly. I purchased all of the books on Africa and the African Diaspora that I could afford. I literally read every day and night. I also attended lectures, seminars and other cultural events relative to Africa and the African experience.

All of this reading had such a profound impact on not only my thinking, but my attitude towards life as well. Things that I previously thought were important were now no longer important to me. What became of paramount importance for me was my own education and the role I could play towards proper education for African American children.

The significance of the aforementioned account of my own personal transformation is that prior to my quest for knowledge of African history, I was just an average student with no real sense of direction and no real sense of purpose in life. As I became a reader of African and African American history however, I simultaneously became a straight "A" student. School simply became less of a challenge for me because in reading the material I was exposing myself to, I was developing a sense of purpose and an amazing sense of intellectual strength and power. In other words, the information I was exposing myself to gave my life new meaning. Studying Malcolm's life provided me with a definition of manhood that was previously absent from my life. What I was reading and exposing myself to was relevant to who I am as an African American man and therefore piqued my interest and curiosity. It enabled me to see myself at the very core of what I was learning. This new education I was receiving was African-centered, which in turn provided me with an African identity. I was exposing myself to information that had historical and cultural relevance for me that I had never been exposed to before. I soon after made the decision that I wanted to devote my life to educating African American children. More specifically, I wanted to share with them what I now knew because I now understood clearly what my purpose was in life.

What does this account have to do with teacher performance in the classroom? It means everything. It is the missing component. It is the mystery that few have been able to decipher relative to African American underachievement and closing the achievement gap. In other words, I too was an African American underachiever. Once I learned my history and culture, my life gained new meaning and academic learning became far less of a challenge because I now had a purpose for learning.

In numerous urban public school classrooms of majority African American student populations throughout the U.S., there is a very noticeable absence of African and African American history, which for the remainder of this chapter, I will refer to as African history with the understanding that I am referring to the entire African Diaspora. Many African American students therefore continue to be exposed to a curriculum where their history, culture, experience, perspectives and interests are either marginalized, distorted or nonexistent. Learning consequently becomes irrelevant, meaningless and undesirable while achievement levels simultaneously plummet and the drop out rates soar. As I stated above, African history for African American students is the missing component.

In the ongoing quest to close the achievement gap between African American and white students, everything has been tried with the exception of the full infusion of

African history into the curricula and African-centered instruction in the classrooms. Although there are pockets of examples in various parts of the country where African-centered instruction is attributable to raising the achievement levels of African American students, it still has not been taken seriously as a viable solution.

In the following section, I will discuss the significance of infusing African history into the curricula and instruction and why it cannot continue to be dismissed or avoided as a viable solution to the wide disparity in achievement between African American and white students.

"Know Thy Self"

Dr. Carter G. Woodson, the founder of what was once called Negro History Week back in February, 1926, which evolved into Black History Month during the 1960's was the author of 16 books. One book in particular, *The Miseducation of the Negro,* written in 1933, is in my judgment, one of the most important books ever written relative to the education of African Americans. Contained in this book is a chapter from which I quote whenever I speak publicly. It states, *"No systematic effort toward change has been possible, for, taught the same economics, history, philosophy, literature and religion which have established the present code of morals, the Negro's mind has been brought under the control of his oppressor. The problem of holding the Negro down, therefore, is easily solved. When you control a man's thinking, you do not have to worry about his actions. You do not have to tell him not to stand here or go yonder. He will find his 'proper place' and will stay in it. You do not need to send him to the back door. He will go without being told. In fact, if there is no back door, he will cut one for his special benefit. His education makes it necessary."*

I have stated numerous times that this paragraph more than epitomizes the plight of the African American community in general and African American children in the public school systems in particular. In other words, African American children continue to be subjected to curricula that is culturally irrelevant which consequently prevents them from instruction and instructional practices that enable them to see themselves at the center of what they are learning. Resultantly, African American children continue to play on a playing field that is not level.

In Ancient Egypt, in which the African name is Kemet, the inscription above the temple entrances read "Know Thy Self." In other words, as far back as four to five thousand years ago, the ancient Egyptians understood the significance of an education that was relevant to who they were and enabled them to gain knowledge and understanding of self.

Up until the time of the European capture and enslavement of the African people, there was a rich tradition of passing the history down through the generations both in writing and orally. African history, culture and tradition was of paramount importance to the African people. The enslavement of the African people virtually erased African history from the memory of the enslaved Africans because there was now no longer anyone to pass it down to through the generations in America due in part to the integration of so many captives of different ethnic (tribal) groups being sold together to the same plantations where language barriers made it virtually impossible to communicate.

Additionally, in order to develop and maintain this system of enslavement, it was expedient from the vantage point of the slave owners to remove all traces of the African tradition from the minds of the enslaved. This was achieved through a system of mental enslavement where over a period of time, enslaved Africans were denied any sense of African history, culture, traditions, languages, names and spiritual worship. Instead they were given an education that said that because they were African, they were inherently inferior to whites and that Africans had made no contributions towards the development of society that was worthy of note. They were taught that being born white meant that you were of a superior being and that whites had created and developed virtually everything imaginable. Even if the enslaved African was fortunate enough to have access to literature that could liberate his mind, the slave laws made it unlawful to teach an enslaved African how to read or write.

This begs the question - why was the tactic of mental enslavement used? The answer is simple. When you can effectively deny a man of his history, you can also effectively deny him of his very humanity. Equally, when you can effectively control the imagery that a man is exposed to, you can also effectively control his mind. After all, slavery could not have been maintained for as long as it was if it had been confined solely to physical enslavement. You had to also enslave the mind if enslavement was going to yield the results that it was intended to produce.

After emancipation from enslavement through 1933 when Woodson wrote the *The Miseducation of the Negro*, the problem of "miseducation" continued to prevail.

Miseducation was so widespread that Woodson among other notable African American scholars devoted their entire lives to researching, studying, writing and teaching the truth about African history.

Although there is a plethora of literature available today regarding African history, systematically teaching it in the schools continues to be problematic. With so much attention being given to Math and Language Arts, little attention is given to the relevance of African American students learning African history and the correlation between knowledge of this history and improvement in achievement. In fact, in my home state of New Jersey, as recently as 2002, legislation had to be passed to ensure that African American enslavement and the middle passage were taught in all of the public schools.

I have argued for the past twenty years that the foundation for African American academic achievement is a firm grounding in African history which can be referred to as the "knowledge of self." In other words, my contention is that the foundation for African American achievement is full exposure to their history and culture. Just as the Egyptian temple entrances read "Know Thy Self," it is absolutely crucial that African American children also "Know Thy Self." They must develop a collective identity through the vehicle of African history which in turn places them at the center of learning and thereby provides them with a purpose for learning.

If one examines the national achievement data of African American students; particularly at the middle school level in urban public schools, what stands out most are the dismal achievement levels in the areas of Math and Language Arts. No matter what school district, state or region of the country, if there are large numbers of African American students, you can almost guarantee that the achievement levels will be disappointing in comparison to white students. This is not a new phenomenon, however. It has persisted throughout the history of public education in this country. No conference, research, study or program has been successful in attacking this problem that did not address African-centered instruction. I contend that no conference, research, study or program will ever be successful in attacking this problem if it does not address African-centered instruction.

Given the amount of money that is allocated annually for reading and math programs for African American students with little or no improvement that is worthy of mention, if one didn't know any better, it could be concluded that there must be something inherently wrong with or inferior about African American children. Of course, we know that this is far from the case. There is nothing inherently wrong with them. The problem is with us; the educators. We have failed to implement appropriate methodology to ensure that African American children achieve academic excellence. African history, coupled with the other principles addressed in this book will increase the probability that the achievement levels of African American children will soar.

Knowledge of self gives African American children the African identity that so many of them lack. By gaining a sense of identity, they in turn develop a sense of purpose. By developing a sense of purpose, their whole attitude towards school and education changes for the better. Their attitude becomes positive. The development of a positive attitude manifests itself in changed behavioral patterns.

Students are then ready to achieve academic excellence. As long as we continue to dismiss or minimize the importance and relevance of African history, African American children will continue to remain at the bottom of the achievement totem pole.

During the enslavement of African Americans, the powers that maintained this system understood clearly that in order to render their captives powerless and to keep them under their control, they must be denied any and all traces of the knowledge of their history. To this day, in school systems across America, we continue to deny African American children the knowledge of their African history.

African-centered Instruction

Frequently, in making the argument for exposure to African history, one might retort that African history is effectively taught during the month of February - Black History Month. It might be felt that since an entire month is being devoted to African history, that the material is being sufficiently covered.

I contend that by singling out a particular month to teach any one subject is nothing more than an add on at best. Teaching a people's history as an add on sends a contradictory message. It sends the message that their history is of little importance and value, and therefore one that can be condensed to a period of one month out of the year. This is why I frequently use the term, African-centered instruction interchangeably with African history. Through African-centered instruction, all of what we teach is taught from the perspective of the African American students in the classroom. For example, in order to bring about educational parity in your classroom, the core subject areas of math, science, language arts and social studies would have to be taught from the vantage point of all of the students; particularly the African American students. An example of this could be the study of the Civil War. In teaching about the Civil War, it is frequently taught using a traditional instructional model which is European American-centered of a war that was fought to save the Union. Little attention is given in earnest to the African-centered perspective regarding what this war really meant to the enslaved and the role played by the African American soldiers towards ultimately freeing themselves.

Traditional instruction as we know it is inherently Eurocentric and consequently biased towards the white students in the classroom; particularly in social studies and history. No argument has to be made that the curriculum and therefore instruction is not culturally relevant to the needs and interests of the African American students. The national achievement data confirms this contention. Resultantly, white American students stand a much greater chance of identifying with the information they are being exposed to because it has cultural relevancy for them only. African Americans on the other hand do not have this luxury. They are expected to be able to adapt to a curriculum and instruction that is culturally irrelevant and culturally inappropriate.

Although many African American children do in fact experience success in this environment, my concern is with the masses of students who do not. It is them who have to struggle with a curriculum and instruction that does not address their reality or experience with the end result being widespread underachievement of African American children.

African-centered instruction on the other hand provides cultural relevancy to learning for African American students. It enables the African American students to see themselves at the center of their learning while simultaneously allowing multiple perspectives to be taught. For example, in teaching math, you would expose your students to the African contribution while utilizing a book such as Claudia Zaslavsky's, *Africa Counts* as a reference. In teaching science, you would expose your students to the African contribution while utilizing a book such as Ivan Van Sertima's, *Blacks in Science* as a reference. In teaching American History, you would expose your students to the African experience in America while utilizing a book such as Molefi Asante's, *A Journey to Liberation* as a reference. In teaching language arts, you would expose your students to the various Harlem Renaissance writers such as Langston Hughes, Zora Neale Hurston, Countee Cullen, Gwendolyn Bennett, James Weldon Johnson, Anne Spencer, Alain Locke, Ida B. Wells-Barnett and Claude McKay.

In classrooms of multiple ethnic groups, the teachers have the added challenge of maintaining a balance for all of their students which is attainable when the commitment to all of the students' educational growth and development are the teachers' number one priority.

Lessons, Models and Examples from African History

African history is replete with lessons, models and examples for African American children to learn, emulate and live by. Through regular exposure to their own history or through the vehicle of African-centered instruction, African American students gain the opportunity to learn from the lessons of the past in order to develop strategies for success for the future.

One of the regular excuses that people use for not investing in opening up their own businesses is a lack of start up capital. Although in most cases this is a very valid reason for not opening a business, there are examples in African American history that prove otherwise. Take for example, Mary McLeod Bethune. She desired to open a school for African American children but had only $1.50 to her name. She didn't let this deter her from her dream, however. With a fierce determination, she worked diligently raising capital so that her dream would one day come true. In October of 1904, her dream of opening a school became her reality. She opened the Daytona Normal and Industrial School in Daytona Beach, Florida which by 1923 became Bethune-Cookman College as a result of a merger with Cookman Institute.

In interviewing people about taking advantage of opportunities, it is not uncommon for one to use their life's circumstances as an excuse for not striving to better themselves. Again, although there may be validity in their excuses, it doesn't mean that the obstacles are so great that they cannot achieve their dreams. Look at the example of Dr. George Washington Carver. Here was a man who was born into slavery but emerged as one of the most important scientists in U.S. history. An agricultural scientist, Carver used the peanut, soybean and sweet potato to make hundreds of different commonly used products such as linoleum, bleach, ink, shaving cream, flour, milk and coffee (instant and dry) through the process of extraction.

Both Bethune and Carver could have created legitimate excuses for not striving to achieve their dreams based upon their circumstances, but they didn't. They both knew and understood who they were as African descendants and rose to unparalleled heights.

African history also serves as a source of pride and inspiration for African American children. Imagine how young African American children would feel about themselves as descendants of Africa knowing that disciplines such as science and technology, astronomy and astrology, architecture and engineering, philosophy and ethics, and mathematics, including calculus, trigonometry, algebra and geometry all originated in Africa. Or imagine how they would feel about themselves as descendants of Africans in America knowing that inventions such as the rail car coupler, the "third rail" of a train track, the induction telegraph system which allows trains to communicate with each another and the central communications station, the refrigerated truck and train, the automatic car wash, automatic transmission of an automobile, the directional signal of an automobile, automatic lubrication of machines and automobiles, the portable X-ray machine, the blood bank, the automatic shoe maker, the automatic traffic signal, the carbon filament contained in light bulbs which allow them to glow and sugar refinery were all created by their ancestors. And finally, imagine how they would feel about themselves as African Americans knowing of the accomplishments made by their ancestors in the areas of education, medicine, business, law, government, civil and human rights, publishing, the military, religion and the arts.

The models, lessons and examples are endless. African

American children simply need maximum exposure to the fullness of the their history from their teachers. As they receive regular instruction in their own history, they can begin to make connections between the past and the present. They can begin to understand that the past is the foundation to the present. Ideally, as a teacher of African American students, you want them to internalize their history and make it a part of who they are so that they ultimately do not make the distinction between their collective past and present. In other words, they need to be able to bridge the gap in order to see that they and their ancestors are one and the same.

As your students are receiving regular exposure to their history through African-centered instruction, the goal is for them to develop a deeper understanding of their roles in the continuum of history. As they learn about Africa's glorious past, then journey through the horrors of enslavement through the struggle for liberation to the present, they must also learn where they fit into the larger picture. They must always be made aware that their existence is attributable to those who struggled before them. They must then learn that they have an obligation to continue that struggle as they pave the way for those coming behind them. Their fight first and foremost is in the classroom. They must understand that as they are striving to achieve academic excellence, they are in turn moving themselves and their people forward.

For those teachers who teach in school systems which remain to be "segregated," all of what has been said thus far should be relatively easy to implement. The larger challenge would be for those teachers who teach in integrated schools or have integrated classrooms. The problem of implementation is not as difficult as it may appear however, because African American children are not the only students that need to be exposed to African history. All students in a given classroom need to be exposed to the history and culture of one another. This raises the consciousness of all of the students in the classroom while building mutual respect between the various ethnic groups as well. The emphasis however should remain to be on significantly exposing all students in the classroom to African history and culture while maintaining a commitment to African-centered instruction.

One must always keep in mind that the African American enslavement experience was the only one in world history where the tactic to maintain it was to dehumanize its victims by "breaking" them spiritually, psychologically, historically, culturally, socially, linguistically, economically, politically and physically. In other words, the goal was to remove from them their dignity. When one examines the national achievement data of African American students in comparison to all other ethnic groups in the U.S., it becomes more than evident that the African American community continues to suffer from the lasting effects of these past atrocities.

The Responsibility of the Teacher

A lot of what you have read in this chapter thus far may or may not be new to you. As a teacher of African American children, where achievement levels continue to rank far below all other ethnic groups in the U.S., it is imperative that your instructional model is African-centered if real connections are going to be made with your students.

You must therefore either be quite knowledgeable of African and African American history and culture or you must become quite knowledgeable. Since you made the decision to become a teacher of African American children, it is your responsibility to learn the history of the students you teach. Until you learn their history, you cannot say that you truly know your students, historically speaking. If you do not know your students, you cannot effectively meet the educational needs of your students. This applies to teachers of all races and ethnicities which include African American teachers. Remember that your responsibility as the classroom teacher is to motivate, educate and empower your students. African history serves as the vehicle towards making this happen.

When I was a classroom teacher, I taught grades 4 - 6. The elementary schools in my district were departmentalized at the time. Social Studies was the subject area that I taught primarily, but I also taught Math and Language Arts over the years. Regardless of the subject area(s) I taught however, my instruction was always African-centered because in my judgment, there was really no other way to make my instruction relevant. As a results-oriented teacher, I obviously had other qualities that made me effective, but I am convinced that the relevancy of what I taught while remaining within the parameters of the district curriculum benefited my students immensely. There is no better feeling than when I see my former students on the street and they thank me for providing them with the "knowledge of self."

As mentioned previously, there are an abundance of books on the market covering all aspects of the African experience. If you are going to effectively meet the educational needs of your African American students, you must immerse yourself into all the literature you can handle on the African American experience. In other words, in order for your students to learn their history, it is you the teacher who must teach it. It is your responsibility, regardless of the subject area(s) you teach to become quite knowledgeable of the history and culture of your students. Additionally, you must also become quite knowledgeable of the African American experience in general which includes arming yourself with literature written specifically for motivating and educating African American children.

In exposing your students to their history and in teaching history in general, you must be careful of not imposing your own biases in your lessons. In teaching history, your role is not to impose your own views, beliefs and opinions of what and who your students should know, respect and appreciate. Your role is to impart information and to guide your students towards reaching their own conclusions through learning how to think critically. For example, my youngest son who is a 5th grader attends an integrated urban public elementary school comprised of African American, Latino, Asian and white students. Recently, he was assigned to write a biographical book report for Black History Month. He chose to write on Malcolm X. His teacher told him that because she was of the opinion that Malcolm X was an advocate of violence, she would not permit his completed report to be displayed on the bulletin board. Although my son was well aware that her opinion was not based on fact, he refrained from challenging her. The problem however is for students in similar situations who accept these opinions because they are coming from their teacher. Consequently, the end result becomes miseducation. Of course, I went to the school the following morning and corrected my son's teacher of her "miseducating."

Remember, the classroom is no place for the imposition of opinions. As a teacher of African American children, it is absolutely crucial that you teach them how to think for themselves.

In a similar situation my oldest son who attends the same school as my youngest son had a social studies lesson last year as a 7th grader where the teacher taught that Abraham Lincoln was a hero to African Americans *because* he "freed the slaves" via the Emancipation Proclamation. Through my son's prior readings and exposure to African American history, he was well aware that the Emancipation Proclamation did not achieve what most people are under the assumption that it did - freeing African Americans from enslavement. In my son's case, he did challenge the teacher, but he did not realize that he had in his possession the documentation to support his contention. When he arrived home, I showed him in his own American History text that the Emancipation Proclamation only offered freedom to the enslaved in those states that Lincoln now had no jurisdiction over - the Confederacy. The border states were permitted to maintain enslavement as long as they remained loyal to the Union. Had the teacher refrained from imposing his own opinion and instead provided the information and led his students to drawing their own conclusions through thinking critically, the students would have had a better opportunity to gain a much more accurate account of this period in history devoid of the bias and opinion of the teacher.

I subsequently instructed my son to return to school

the next day with the confidence to respectfully challenge the contention of his teacher, utilizing his American History text and one of my books entitled, *Africa's Gift to America* by J. A. Rogers.

Following is a list of books that I recommend all teachers of African American children read and study immediately in an effort to expand your knowledge base of the African American experience. This is not intended to be an exhaustive nor comprehensive list, but it is representative of the type of reading that teachers of African American children must engage in.

In locating these titles, be mindful that throughout the history of the U.S., it has always been difficult to get some of the more progressive literature that is written by African American authors published, distributed and sold through the main stream outlets. This required African Americans to create our own publishing, distribution and retail network which I am proud to say that I have been a part of for over a decade. With that being said, some of the books listed may be difficult to locate. All of these books can be located in virtually any Black Bookstore, however. If you have problems locating one, you can type in the titles or authors on any Internet search engine and you shouldn't have a problem.

Suggested Reading

African History

1. Black Man of the Nile - Yosef ben-Jochannan
2. Introduction to African Civilizations - John G. Jackson
3. The African Origins of Civilization - Cheik Anta Diop
4. The Cultural Unity of Black Africa - Cheik Anta Diop
5. Stolen Legacy - George G. M. James
6. Destruction of Black Civilization - Chancellor Williams
7. World's Great Men of Color, Vols. I and II - J. A. Rogers
8. Sex and Race, Vols. I-III - J. A. Rogers
9. Nile Valley Contributions to Civilization -
      Anthony T. Browder
10. Nile Valley Civilizations - Ivan Van Sertima

African-American History

1. Before the Mayflower - Lerone Bennett, Jr.
2. From Slavery to Freedom - John Hope Franklin
3. Notes For An African World Revolution -
      John Henrik Clarke
4. African American History - A Journey to Liberation
      Molefi Kete Asante
5. How Europe Underdeveloped Africa - Walter Rodney
6. They Came Before Columbus - Ivan Van Sertima
7. Blacks in Science - Ivan Van Sertima
8. Black Inventors of America - McKinley Burt, Jr.
9. Great Negroes: Past and Present - Russell Adams
10. Introduction to Black Studies - Maulana Karenga
11. What They Never Told You in History Class - Kush
12. Peculiar Institution - Kenneth Stampp
13. Africa's Gift to America - J. A. Rogers
14. Philosophy and Opinions of Marcus Garvey -
      Amy Jacques Garvey
15. Marcus Garvey, Hero - Tony Martin
16. Marcus Garvey and the Vision of Africa -
      John Henrik Clarke
17. Up From Slavery - Booker T. Washington
18. Life and Times of Frederick Douglass -
      Frederick Douglass
19. Harriet Tubman - Ann Petry

20. Autobiography of W. E. B. DuBois
21. Autobiography of Malcolm X - Alex Haley
22. Malcolm X Speaks - George Brietman
23. Malcolm X, The Man and His Times -
    John Henrik Clarke
24. King, A Biography - David Lewis

Teaching African American Students
1. A Talk With Jawanza - Jawanza Kunjufu
2. Black Students/Middle Class Teachers - Jawanza Kunjufu
3. Black Children - Janice Hale
4. Learning While Black - Janice Hale
5. Marva Collins Way - Marva Collins
6. Ordinary Children/Extraordinary Teachers -
    Marva Collins
7. I Choose To Stay - Salome Thomas-El
8. Black Teachers on Teaching - Michele Foster
9. From Rage to Hope:
    Strategies for Reclaiming Black and Hispanic Students -
    Crystal Kuykendall

Motivating / Inspiring African American Students
1. Awakening the Natural Genius of Black Children -
    Amos N. Wilson
2. Developing Positive Self-Images and
    Discipline in Black Children - Jawanza Kunjufu
3. To Be Popular or Smart: The Black Peer Group -
    Jawanza Kunjufu
4. Harvesting New Generations:
    The Positive Development of Black Youth -
    Useni E. Perkins

Connecting With African American Males
1. Countering the Conspiracy to
    Destroy Black Boys, Vols. I-IV - Jawanza Kunjufu
2. Bringing the Black Boy to Manhood: The Hare Plan -
    Nathan and Julia Hare
3. Educating African American Males:
    Detroit's Malcolm X Academy Solution -
    Clifford Watson and Geneva Smitherman

29

4. Coming of Age - Paul Hill

Psychology
1. Developmental Psychology of the Black Child - Amos N. Wilson
2. Chains and Images of Psychological Slavery - Na'im Akbar

Other Important Titles
1. Miseducation of the Negro - Carter G. Woodson
2. Afrocentricity - Molefi Kete Asante
3. Black Students Guide to Positive Education - Zak Kondo
4. African Centered Rites of Passage and Education - Lathardus Goggins II
5. Issues in African American Education - Walter Gill
6. For the Children - Madeline Cartwright
7. Africa Counts - Claudia Zaslavsky
8. Infusion of African and African American Content in the School Curriculum -
   Asa G. Hilliard III
   Lucretia Payton-Stewart
   Larry Obadele Williams
9. A Black Parent's Handbook to Educating Your Children (Outside of the Classroom) - Baruti K. Kafele
10. A Black Student's Guide to Goal Setting - Baruti K. Kafele

References

1. Adams, Russell. (1963). *Great Negroes, Past and Present.* Chicago: Afro-Am Publishing Co., Inc.

2. Asante, Molefi K. (1988). *Afrocentricity.* Trenton: Africa World Press, Inc.

3. Burt, Jr., McKinley. (1969). *Black Inventors of America.* Portland: National Book Company.

4. Rogers, J. A. (1961). *Africa's Gift to America.* St. Petersburg: Helga M. Rogers.

5. Van Sertima, Ivan. (1983). *Blacks in Science.* New Brunswick and London: Transaction Books.

6. Woodson, Carter G. (1933). *The Miseducation of the Negro.* Hakim's Publications: Philadelphia.

2.   A MINDSET FOR TEACHING

There are a variety of different reasons that teachers have as to why they entered the teaching profession, which could be summarized into three broad categories. The first category of teachers who represent the majority of today's teachers entered teaching as a result of making a decision very early in their lives that they wanted to make a difference in the lives of children and therefore spend their careers as teachers. They in turn majored in some area of education in a college or university program and subsequently became classroom teachers. The second category of teachers decided at some point while working in some other occupation that they could find more self fulfillment as a teacher while at the same time making a difference in the lives of children. They therefore took the required courses and/or exams and entered the teaching profession through an alternate program. The third category of teachers simply needed employment, but were not necessarily aspiring teachers. Classroom teaching positions were available so they took advantage of the opportunity. They may have already possessed the preliminary credentials to enter the teaching profession such as a Bachelors Degree. They therefore took the required examination and entered the teaching profession through an alternate program as well. Of course, there are many other individual reasons as to why individuals enter into teaching, but again the aforementioned represents a broad summary.

In addition to the various reasons for entering the teaching profession, there are also various reasons for selecting a particular area of concentration such as teaching on the elementary level versus the secondary level; teaching Regular Ed. versus Special Ed.; teaching algebra versus science; teaching in an urban school district versus a suburban school district or teaching in a large school versus a small school. Once the decision to enter teaching has been made and an area of concentration has been selected, it is absolutely crucial that you develop a clearly defined purpose for your practice of teaching African American children.

Defining Your Purpose

In teaching, as with other professions, you must have a purpose for what you do. Your purpose drives everything you say and everything you do in the classroom as the teacher. The absence of a purpose translates into a teacher with no particular aim, focus or direction. A teacher with no aim, focus or direction translates into students with little opportunity for success.

In defining your purpose for teaching, you should first be ever so mindful of the wide disparity in achievement between African American and white students. Inherent in your overall purpose for teaching must therefore be to close the achievement gap through the students you teach by striving to ensure that all of your students achieve academic excellence. All of your instructional activities must therefore be rooted in your overall purpose for teaching. Secondly, in defining your purpose for teaching, it is not enough to simply say for example, that "I want to change the lives of young people." Your purpose must be much more comprehensive which includes where it is that you want to take your students, what it is you expect them to know and achieve, and why you consider this to be important.

When I was a classroom teacher, I primarily taught social studies. My purpose for teaching was to teach my students about the principles of socioeconomic development while instilling in them a mindset towards the eventual control of their own communities using the vehicle of African history and culture. My academic expectation was for all of my students to achieve academic excellence.

As a teacher of African American students who resided in an urban community that was predominantly African American, I understood clearly the need for my students to develop a sense for socioeconomic development and control of the communities in which they live. I also understood that in order for them to firmly understand and appreciate their roles towards the future socioeconomic development and control of their community, they must first be firmly rooted and grounded in African history and culture. I considered learning African history and culture important because it puts the current plight of African American socioeconomic development and control in a historical context. This then became my foundation for teaching. It drove everything I said and did as the teacher of my students. In other words, this was my purpose for entering the teaching profession.

To this day, despite the fact that my classroom teaching has evolved into the principalship, parent training, motivational speaking, consulting and writing, my initial purpose for teaching continues to be what drives me today. In fact, there are three key words that underscore what I do as an educator. They are, to *motivate, educate* and *empower*. As teachers, your focus must also be to consistently *motivate*, *educate* and *empower* your students which sums up what we all should be striving to do as educators.

I think it is a fair assumption to make that consensus will never be reached towards defining a universal purpose for teaching African American children. What is most important however, is that all classroom teachers of African American students determine a purpose for teaching that is rooted first in their students achieving academic excellence and second, in their students developing an understanding and an appreciation for their roles and responsibilities towards building, developing and controlling the communities in which they live. In other words, "planting the seeds" for economic self sufficiency and entrepreneurship.

Entering the classroom each and every day devoid of a clearly defined purpose for being there is detrimental to the educational growth and development of the students you teach. This particularly holds true for the third broad category of teachers referenced earlier, ie. those who entered the profession because they needed employment and are therefore not aspiring teachers. For these individuals, developing a purpose for teaching is absolutely essential if their students stand any real chance for achieving excellence.

It is critically important that both new and aspiring teachers enter the teaching profession with a clearly defined purpose for teaching from the outset. It is equally important however that veteran teachers have a clearly defined purpose for teaching as well. For a variety of reasons, many veteran teachers have lost the passion and enthusiasm they once had for teaching. Having a purpose for teaching helps to restore that lost passion and enthusiasm. It enables teachers to maintain their sense of focus and commitment while simultaneously preventing distractions from becoming the prevailing focus.

Being Mission-Driven

Your purpose for teaching translates into your mission. In other words, as a classroom teacher, you must be on a mission to ensure that all of your students achieve academic excellence. You must develop a "nothing will stop my students from achieving excellence" attitude. Your mission, coupled with your purpose then drives everything you say and do as a classroom teacher.

When I was a classroom teacher, I was on a definite mission. My mission started with me giving my classroom a name. Over my classroom door was a sign that read, "The Mind Zone." "The Mind Zone" was reflective of my overall mission and the mission of the class. Once my students entered the room, they would see a banner that read, "The Mind Zone - Where Minds are Transformed into Greatness!" When my students entered the classroom, they knew that they were in a mission-driven environment. My mission, as they knew, was to do all that was within my power to ensure that my students achieved academic excellence. As with my purpose, my mission drove all that I said and did as their teacher every day.

As a teacher of African American students, you too must approach your practice of teaching with a strong sense of mission. Everything that you say and everything that you do becomes inspired by your sense of mission which again is rooted in your overall purpose for teaching.

Your mission must also be conveyed to your students both verbally and by your actions. Your actions will dictate to your students whether or not you are actually serious and committed to their educational growth and development.

Your mission must then translate into an intense determination and a burning desire to see your students achieve academic excellence. When you possess an intense determination and a burning desire to see your students achieve academic excellence, the probability for their success increases dramatically.

Using the example of sports; before the game begins, athletes usually use some form of a routine or ritual for getting themselves "pumped" for the game. Some strategies used include yelling positive affirmations, high-fiving each other, jumping up and down, meditating, listening to motivational music or listening to and processing the coach's motivational message. This in turn gets the athletes "pumped" before going out onto the field or court. As a classroom teacher, you too must be "pumped" before entering the classroom. You must develop some kind of routine that works for you to get you "pumped" for the prospects of each day. You want to enter your classroom each and every day with an intense determination and burning desire to fulfill your mission as your students' teacher.

Having a Vision

In defining a purpose for teaching, one must also develop an overall vision for where you see yourself as a teacher over a period of time and where you see your students over a period of time. Your vision provides you with a long range target to aim for.

Do you ever consider where you will be relative to your own professional development and success over a 5, 10, 15 year period? As a teacher, you must always strive to grow in your profession. Staying stagnant will have an adverse effect on your students. If you are not growing and staying current with the latest educational research and trends, your students become victims of a teacher that is utilizing outdated and obsolete methodologies and practices to teach the youth of today. You must therefore strive to grow and develop with time. Before you begin this process however, you must envision where it is that you want to be or what it is that you want to become over a definite period of time. In other words, you must develop and maintain a sense of vision. You must be able to see yourself as a master teacher with all of your students achieving academic excellence. You must also be able to envision the things you will have to do in order to make your vision become your reality.

During my first year as a classroom teacher, I decided that I wanted to one day become the district teacher of the year. I therefore not only made this a goal, but I envisioned myself achieving this fete within the next five years. I then worked assiduously to convert my vision into my reality. I read all I could get my hands on relative to my practice of teaching and I attended professional development workshops often. In my classroom, I continued to implement strategies which would increase the probability for student success. By doing all of the things I set out to do, at the end of my fourth year, I was selected as the school, district and county teacher of the year. My vision became my reality. This translated into high student achievement amongst the majority of the students I taught.

Visionary teachers are not complacent with their current teaching skills and ability; despite the successes they may be currently experiencing. Visionary teachers can see themselves years from now as master teachers or as super teachers. They understand that as they improve, their students' chances for success also improves. On the other hand, teachers without a vision are probably not cognizant of the fact that their lack of vision can adversely impact their students' ability to grow. In meeting the educational needs of African American children, it is imperative that they are given the opportunity to have teachers who are visionary and therefore envision themselves growing, developing and evolving into master teachers.

In addition to having a vision for yourself, you must also have a vision for your students. You must possess a vision for where you see your students at the end of each marking period and at the end of the school year. Your marking period and year-end vision provides you with a road map to follow. On the other hand, if you have no vision for your students, you have no clue or idea of where you expect them to be over a period of time.

Once you've developed a vision for your students, you'll need to share your vision with them. They need to know that their teacher has a vision for their success. Making meaningful connections with your students becomes that much more realistic when they know that their teacher has a vision for their educational growth and development.

Setting Incremental Goals

As you are determining and assessing your overall

vision for yourself and your students, you will also need to set incremental goals. Picture in your mind a staircase with each step representing a goal and the top step representing your vision. As you climb the staircase and therefore achieve each of your incremental goals, you are getting that much closer to fulfilling your vision.

Your incremental goals should always be written and posted in some visible area where you will see them on a regular basis. If you are really daring, you can post your goals in your classroom so that your students and colleagues can see them as well. When your goals are posted in a high visibility area such as your classroom, it becomes much more difficult to quit when the pursuit of your goals becomes challenging. When others are aware of your goals, they are in a position to assist you towards achieving them. Who better to assist you and keep you focused than your students and your colleagues?

In setting your goals, you'll want to consider the whole of your practice of teaching and set goals for improvement in various categories, such as the number of professional development workshops in a specific area you will attend during the year; the number of professional books and journals you will read during the year; the number of students achieving academic distinction per marking period / year; the number of students achieving student of the month per month / year; the number of students reading 25 books or more over the course of the year; the number of behavioral infractions and distractions per month / year with the vision being to eliminate them, and the number of parent contacts you will make per month / year. Of course, this list is by no means exhaustive. It is meant to provide you with a starting point towards setting goals that are consistent with your overall purpose, mission and vision as a teacher.

After your goals have been written, you must then develop a strategy for achieving them. It's easy to say you are going to achieve whatever it is that you desire to achieve. The true challenge is developing a plan of action and then adhering to that plan.

In devising your plan of action, a format you can follow is one I developed called the "Goal Chart." It is comprised of the following three sections: Current Standing, Goals and Strategy.

In the current standing section of your goal chart, you would write either a listing or a narrative of where you currently stand towards the achievement of your goals. Your current standing answers the question, "Where am I now?" As one who is pursuing goals, before doing anything else, you must first determine where it is that you currently stand before embarking on moving forward.

In the goals section of your goal chart, you would write your actual goals for the school year or for specific periods of time within the school year. Your goals answer the question, "Where am I going?" Again, you could either write your goals as a listing or you could write them as a narrative. With each of the goals that you set, be sure to also set a time frame for when you expect to achieve them.

In the third section of your goal chart, you would write your strategy for achieving the goals that you set in the goals section. Your strategy answers the question, "How am I going to get there?" Your strategy should be written as a detailed plan of action.

Again, your completed goal chart should be posted in some visible area to enable you to review on an ongoing basis. On the following page is an outline of a completed goal chart.

Your Name

I. Current Standing

II. Goals

III. Strategy

In Chapter Three - Motivating Your Students, I will provide a much more detailed account on assisting your students with setting their own goals for each of the marking periods of the school year.

Setting the Example - Modeling Expected Outcomes

Towards solidifying your purpose which includes your mission, vision and incremental goals, remember that what you say and what you do will actually determine who you are in the eyes of your students. This means that there cannot be any contradictions between your purpose, mission and vision, and your actions. Consistency must prevail.

As a teacher of African American students, you have a great responsibility to fulfill. For 180 days, you are the leader, example and model for your students. Your success as their teacher will determine the direction you lead them in. If you are successful as their teacher, you can conclude that you have led them in the right direction. If on the other hand you are unsuccessful as their teacher, you can conclude that you have not effectively led them. For African American children in urban public schools, your successful or unsuccessful leadership could determine their life's chances. You must therefore strive to be an effective teacher in all aspects of classroom teaching.

As a teacher of African American students, you are a role model whether you want to be or not. Your students will closely assess your every word and your every move. You must therefore lead by example. You must model expected behavior and conduct at all times. Following are areas that should receive special attention.

A. Oral Communication

In a typical urban public school, standard English amongst African American students in their normal interactions with their peers or teachers is not necessarily the norm. This is not a wholesale indictment of non-standard English however. Non-standard English or even "ebonics" has its place in African American culture which is well beyond the scope of this book. My criticism is when students cannot make the transition from non-standard English to standard English. This subsequently manifests itself when students engage in writing. More frequently than not, African American students have difficulty with English grammar in writing because of the problems they have with standard English in speaking. This means that teachers must be conscious of their role in modeling standard English in their oral communication with their students at all times. When classroom teachers are of the rationale that they will speak to the students in "their language" in an effort to relate with them, the teachers' intentions are probably good but to the detriment of their students learning how to speak standard English. Teachers must therefore model the kind of communication that they expect from their students. If on the other hand, teachers lack the ability to speak standard English, they have no place in the teaching profession teaching children.

B. Written Communication

As with oral communication, teachers must be cognizant of their own written communication that is read by their students. When writing on the chalkboard or white board for example, the information written must be grammatically correct. When teachers write sentences on the board, they are once again modeling expected outcomes. Teachers must therefore be conscious of the fact that when grammatically incorrect sentences are written on the board, failure is inadvertently being modeled for their students. As students are held accountable for sentence construction, content organization, usage and mechanics in their own writing, teachers must also be cognizant of their roles in modeling the kind of writing that will increase the probability that their students will become proficient writers.

C. Attire

Towards setting an example for your students, you must also consider the attire you wear to school. True professionals wear professional attire because they understand that they are modeling professionalism for their students. I have always considered the school to be a professional environment comprised of professional educators. As professional educators, you must always dress professionally. When you come to work to teach in unprofessional attire, you send the message to your students that professionalism is not important which in turn detracts from the way that you are seen, perceived and respected by your students. I have observed far too often that students will not take their teachers seriously if anything less than professionalism is presented. Attention must therefore be devoted to your impression of how you may be perceived by your students.

As a professional educator, you must always be conscious of your purpose for teaching. As a teacher of African American children, your focus must be the goal of all of your students achieving academic excellence. In addition to the academic side of teaching, you must also be conscious of your role regarding the social development of your students. If you are going to be effective in shaping and molding your students both academically and socially, you must have credibility in the eyes of your students. Your students must therefore see you as nothing less than a true professional who is the holder of the keys to their success. When you come to school for example, in jeans, polo shirts, flannel shirts, overalls, sports jerseys, sweat shirts, sweat pants and sneakers, you make it very difficult for your students to embrace you as a true professional, despite whatever content area expertise you may possess. Moreover, when you come to school dressed in this manner, you relinquish your authority to provide your students with proper guidance and leadership relative to their own attire.

Towards developing the whole student, it would be ideal that you have a dress code for your classroom which includes the following:

- All dress shirts and blouses must be fully buttoned.
- All undershirts must be tucked in.
- All pants must be pulled up to the waist.
- All shoe and sneaker laces must be tied.
- All shorts, skirts and dresses must be of an appropriate length for school.
- No provocative apparel permitted.
- No gang-related paraphernalia permitted.
- No headbands, hats, wave caps or scarves permitted.

If your attire is less than professional, it will be very difficult for you to uphold a classroom student dress code.

Conversely, when you come to school in professional attire such as a shirt, tie, slacks and shoes for men and best professional attire for women, the probability that your students will perceive, treat and respect you as a professional increases. The key is that as a professional, you must always model for your students what you expect of them. Again, your purpose for teaching must go far beyond the academic side of the students solely and expand to address the whole student.

D. Punctuality and Attendance

You can't consider yourself to be a true professional if you are frequently late for school or class. Your students are dependent upon you reporting to work on time every day. When your students are late for school or late for class, you in all probability hold them accountable for their tardiness. When they see you arriving to school late or arriving to class late, they wonder how it is and why it is that a double standard exists. As a professional educator modeling expected behaviors for your students, you must arrive to school and class on time every day.

The same holds true for attendance. Outside of the times when you are under the weather, your students are dependent upon you reporting to school every day. When your students are absent, chances are good that you hold them accountable for all the work they missed. When you are absent, the students miss a full day of instruction from their teacher. You must therefore strive to report to work everyday of the school year to increase the probability that your students will receive 180 full days of instruction from their own teachers.

Self-Reflection and Self-Assessment

Thus far, we have examined defining a purpose for teaching, being mission-driven, having a vision, setting incremental goals and setting an example for your students. In this section, I will discuss the importance of self-reflection and self-assessment.

Every morning upon waking up for work, before getting completely out of bed, it is good practice to sit at the foot of your bed and envision your day. Think about the lessons you plan to teach, the activities you plan to engage your students in, the things you have to do and the things you want to accomplish. Set little mental goals for yourself. Tell yourself that you will accomplish them, and tell yourself that you are going to have your best day yet. In other words, each and every morning, you want to get yourself mentally prepared and motivated for the challenges of the day. Once this process is complete, proceed with your normal morning routine.

At the end of the day, after all of the students have left the building, return to your desk and sit down. Close your eyes and reflect upon the entire day from start to finish while refraining from doing any assessing or judging. Reflect upon both your successes and failures and reflect upon anything that may have been unusual. Consider your interactions with students, colleagues, parents and administration. The key is reflecting upon all that occurred from start to finish. You should also record your thoughts in a reflection journal so that you can make reference to them at some later date. Each day that you write in your reflection journal, be sure to write the current date.

After you have completed reflecting, you should then

begin to assess your day. In other words, now you want to determine what worked and what failed. For those practices that worked, you'll want to determine why. For those practices that didn't work, you'll want to determine why not. As you are assessing your day, you should also be recording your assessment in your reflection journal. Additionally, you should develop a brief plan in your journal for what you could have done differently for those practices that were ineffective. For example, maybe you didn't challenge a student hard enough that gave an incorrect answer during guided questioning. During your assessment, you might determine that a different line of questioning may have elicited a better response from your student. You will then make the proper adjustments for the next lesson. The key here is disciplining yourself to always reflect upon your day while assessing what worked and what was ineffective. Again, it is best that you record your thoughts in a reflection journal so that you can make reference to your writing at some later date. Additionally, be sure to date each day's writing and clearly distinguish your reflection from your assessment by labeling both. This whole process should take no more than fifteen minutes.

Keep in mind that there are going to be days when by day's end you are going to wonder if anything went right at all. There will be days when nothing seems to work and consequently, little or no learning takes place. I call days like this the knock-out punch. In other words, the experiences of the day were comparable to a boxer getting knocked out in the ring. When you have days like this, you like the boxer, have received the knock-out punch. The question is, how long will it take for you to get up and get back on your feet? Are you going to stay down or will you get right back up; stronger than ever? During your assessment of the day when you are determining what went wrong and what you could have done differently, you must determine what it is that you will do better for the next school day in order to redeem yourself as the teacher and to allow your students the opportunity to learn and achieve. Your students cannot afford for you to stay on the canvas. You must get up and return to school the next day stronger than ever.

The next morning when you begin to envision your day, be sure to incorporate what was reflected upon and assessed the day prior. Remember that your self-reflection and self-assessment should always be consistent with your overall purpose, mission and vision.

3. MOTIVATING YOUR STUDENTS

If you have taught for at least one day, you are well aware of the fact that you must have the attention of your students if you are going to be successful as their teacher. Once you have gained their attention, you must have the ability to hold on to it by keeping your students motivated and focused. If you do not have the ability to motivate your students, you will not be able to effectively educate them. Discipline will soon become your focus while learning becomes secondary. In meeting the educational needs of African American children, keeping them motivated and focused is unavoidable if they are are going to achieve academic excellence in your classroom. The focus of this chapter will therefore be on keeping your students motivated.

The Five Key Ingredients for Success

For many years, I have argued that in order to be successful in any walk of life, there are certain "ingredients" that one must possess. Think about baking a homemade cake for example. A homemade cake contains many different ingredients and each one plays a role towards making a good cake. With any one ingredient missing, the cake will be less than optimal because all of the ingredients are not in place.

The same holds true in motivating your students where it is essential that all of the necessary ingredients are in place. I have maintained for many years that at a minimum, these ingredients are: belief, purpose, obligation, determination and vision, meaning that as your students are learning their history and making it a part of who they are, through your regular and ongoing encouragement, you should be helping them to develop a strong belief in their ability to achieve, a meaningful sense of purpose, a firm understanding of their obligation to achieve academic excellence, an intense determination to succeed and an overall sense of vision for where they expect to see themselves over a period of time. I will now discuss each ingredient individually.

A. Belief

The first key ingredient for success is belief. In order for your students to achieve academic excellence, it is essential that they believe that they have the ability to do so. If they lack belief in themselves, chances are good that they will not achieve at the level that you expect them to achieve.

You must remind your students constantly that you believe in them and that they must also believe in themselves. They must earnestly believe that they possess the ability to achieve academic excellence in your classroom. If on the other hand they do not believe in their abilities to become successful, chances are good that they will not experience success.

As you are striving to build connections between your students and their history, it is essential that you expose them to the numerous individuals in African American history that experienced success in their respective fields of endeavor. You must teach your students that the accomplishments of these individuals were rooted in their belief in their ability to become successful. African American children need to understand that they too must first believe firmly in their abilities to achieve success. As the old adage goes, if you can conceive it and believe it; you can achieve it.

The key is reminding and encouraging your students constantly to believe that they do in fact have the ability to achieve academic excellence so that over a period of time, their accomplishments become reflective of their belief in themselves.

B. Purpose

The second key ingredient for success is purpose. Just as the classroom teacher must have a purpose for teaching, students must have a purpose for learning. Your students' sense of purpose begins with them making a determination as to why they are in school in the first place. Through observing and interviewing students over the years, I have come to the realization that many of them are unsuccessful in part because they do not have a purpose for attending school that goes beyond "to get an education." Your students must understand that the purpose of school is to learn, which will enable them to lay a solid foundation for productivity in later years.

As African Americans students, their purpose for attending school must include the attainment of academic excellence. In the context of the African American community as a whole, their purpose must relate to the overall growth and development of the African American community. It is your role to help them make the connection between achievement in the classroom, and the socioeconomic development of their community. They must be able to see this relationship and therefore make the connection between the two. As this connection is being made and your students gain a deeper understanding of their roles towards the socioeconomic development of their communities, a stronger and more meaningful sense of purpose can emerge.

Frequently, we will ask children what they want to be when they grow up. A student may respond that he wants to become a doctor which in turn becomes his purpose for attending school. For this particular student, you must be able to keep him focused on his purpose. You must also be able to show him the relationship between his purpose and the potential impact he can later make in the African American community. He must come to believe that through a strong sense of commitment to his purpose, he may one day be the one who discovers the cure for cancer, AIDS or any of the other ailments that continue to devastate the African American community for example. The key is that all of your students must have a purpose for learning as a component of keeping them motivated towards their education.

C. Obligation

The third key ingredient for success is obligation. African American students have to be made to understand that being born African American places on them certain responsibilities. They have to be made to understand that their very existence coupled with the opportunities they have been afforded to achieve their dreams are a direct result of the struggles waged by those who came before them. In other words, the reality is that they are descendants of a people who were not long ago enslaved in the Americas. The freedom that all African Americans now experience is a result of the dedication and sacrifices of millions of people before them.

You must teach your students that it is now their turn. They need to understand that they must continue the struggle that started with the commencement of enslavement. They must be made aware that this struggle is by no means over but that it continues and is manifested in the latest national achievement data of African American students for example. In other words, African American children are obligated to continue to struggle for justice and equality. Their fight however is not in the streets and courtrooms. Their fight is in the classroom. By striving to achieve academic excellence, they are doing their part in this monumental effort. They are demonstrating the ability of African American children to achieve excellence in the classroom and therefore laying a foundation and paving the way for others to follow. The key however is for you the classroom teacher to make your students fully aware that in the context of the socioeconomic growth and development of the African American community, they have an obligation to strive for excellence as a component of keeping them motivated towards their education.

D. Determination

The fourth key ingredient for success is determination. You must encourage your children to have a burning desire to achieve academic excellence. They must be intensely determined to settle for nothing less than meeting and exceeding your expectations for them to succeed.

We all know of people who were pursuing some dream and as soon as obstacles, challenges or the negativity of others set in, they decided to quit. The goal was no longer important to them. They had become sidetracked by surmountable obstacles or influences. In other words, they did not have a burning desire to succeed. They lacked the necessary determination.

Your job is to keep your students determined for success in the classroom. In order for your students to maintain success, their determination must be sustained over the course of the school year. If you are successful in keeping them determined, the probability for academic excellence increases. The key then is keeping them determined as a component of keeping them motivated towards their education.

E. Vision

In my discussion of developing a purpose for teaching, I discussed the importance of having a vision for where you see yourself over a period of time. The same holds true for your students. They too must have a vision for where they expect to see themselves over a period of time. Again, they must be able to make the connection between school and the socioeconomic development of their community. This requires having a vision.

Additionally, your students must have a vision relative to their academic accomplishments. They must have vision for their marking period accomplishments, their year long accomplishments, their elementary and secondary school accomplishments and ultimately graduating from college. They must be able to envision themselves being successful before actually embarking on accomplishing their goals.

A good exercise towards getting your students to dream and develop a vision for success is at the start of each marking period, have them sit at their desks and close their eyes. With their eyes closed, tell them to visualize the auditorium or wherever your quarterly student achievement recognition assemblies usually take place. Tell them to see themselves walking across the stage receiving their Honor Roll certificates from their principal. With their eyes still closed ask them can they see themselves receiving this honor. Then ask them if it makes them feel good. Then repeat the process with graduation from whatever level school you teach. Finally, repeat the process with graduation from college. Once you have completed this process, tell them that they have actually accomplished all they had envisioned by seeing themselves already successful. Let them know that now all they have to do is work hard each and every day to make their vision become their reality.

As mentioned above, these five key ingredients must be present at all times as components of keeping your students motivated towards achieving success. It is your responsibility to continually keep your students focused on incorporating all five in an effort of keeping them motivated towards achieving academic excellence.

The Blueprint for Success

As you are striving to keep your students motivated towards achieving academic excellence, you will also need to teach your students about the importance of, and how to go about setting goals and developing strategies to achieve them. You must then hold your students accountable for actually setting their goals and working towards achieving them.

When students set goals for themselves, they have targets to aim for. They have predetermined exactly what it is that they are going to achieve. When goals are not set, students have no targets to aim for. Consequently, they wind up wandering aimlessly with no real sense of direction or focus. With achievement levels being where they are relative to the achievement gap, African American children cannot afford to wander aimlessly. They need to set goals that are concrete, specific, attainable, short range and long range.

A. Concrete Goals

In setting goals, your students need to set goals that are concrete, meaning that they are clearly defined, written down and visibly posted.

In academic goal setting, what I mean by a clearly defined goal is a letter grade goal in each of the individual subject areas. The goal would be that specific grade that the student expects to earn, such as an "A." You would never say, for example, that your goal is to achieve an "A" *or* a "B." Setting goals as one goal or the other lets the student off of the hook if the higher goal is not attained. The objective is to therefore strive for the one specific grade in each subject area while always working hard to exceed the goals that were set.

Concrete goals are always written. A memorized goal can always be forgotten. It is also easy to change a memorized goal. Written goals are much harder to change and serve as a constant reminder for your students that they are in pursuit of achieving their goals.

Lastly, concrete goals are always posted in some visible area where your students will be able to see them and review them on a regular basis.

B. Attainable Goals

An attainable goal is a goal that can be realistically achieved based upon where one currently stands towards their own particular development. The operative word here is "realistic." You must be able to guide your students towards setting goals that are realistic so that they don't make the mistake of setting themselves up for failure in the event that they are unsuccessful towards achieving the goals that were set.

On the other hand, your students should be discouraged from setting goals that do not pose a real challenge. If your students do not challenge themselves through setting goals that are challenging yet attainable, they are not challenging themselves to grow. In setting goals, the aim must always be progress and improvement. Once a particular goal is achieved such as a "B" in math, the new goal must be to achieve an "A." You would never set the same goal again until the goal of "A," which is the highest goal, has been achieved.

C. Short-Range/Long Range Goals

Goals are usually broken down into short-range and long-range. In the context of academic goals, the short-range goals would be the grades that your students are striving to achieve on tests, quizzes, projects, papers and marking period grades. The long-range goals would be the final grade, final grade point average or graduation. Your students' short-range goals are the stair steps that take them to the top of the staircase - their long-range goals, which comprise their overall vision.

D. The Goal Chart

When I was an undergraduate college student, I studied Marketing. One of the first principles that I learned in my marketing classes was that in marketing a product or service, you must have an organized, systematic plan of action. If you had no organized, systematic plan, you were destined for failure. The plan enabled you to organize your activities and provided you with a format and framework that told you everything you needed to do to ultimately profit from your product or service. In setting student academic goals, they too will need organized, systematic plans to keep them on track and focused. This plan is called "The Goal Chart."

The goal chart is a three part plan which is comprised of the Current Standing section, the Goals section and the Strategy section. As it is imperative that goals are set before embarking on any new project or undertaking, each of your students should prepare a goal chart on the first day of school and the day after report card distribution at the start of each marking period. Following I will discuss the development of your students' goal charts for teachers of self-contained classes and goal cards for teachers of departmentalized classes.

E. Current Standing

The first section of the goal chart is called the "Current Standing" section. This section answers the question, "Where am I now?" In other words, the current standing section of the goal chart is your students' starting point for setting their marking period goals. Keeping in mind that you can't move forward until you know where you are coming from, the current standing section of the goal chart serves as a reminder to your students of where they currently stand and provides a basis for setting new marking period goals.

In setting up the goal chart, as I stated previously, everything must be written down so that it can eventually be posted and reviewed regularly. On sheets of lined notebook paper, in the center of the first line, have your students write their first names in large capital letters next to the word - GOALS. Beneath their names, they should write the marking period number they are currently in, ie. 1st Marking Period. Beneath the marking period number, on the left hand side of the page, they should write the subheading - Current Standing. Beneath current standing, they should list each of their subjects and write their current grades beside each. If you are at the start of the first marking period of a new school year, each of your students is starting with a clean slate. You can therefore either bypass the current standing section for this marking period only or you can start all students with an "A" average while encouraging them to work hard to maintain their "A" average. Keep in mind also that in marking period number two, the actual report card grades will comprise the current standing section. You may therefore want to inform your principal and your students' parents that you plan to post current grades as a basis for the next marking periods' goals.

On the other hand, if you opt not to use the current standing portion of the goal chart in your classroom, you can encourage your students' parents to utilize it in their homes. On the following page is a sample outline of the current standing section of the goal chart.

BARUTI'S GOALS

Marking Period #2

<u>Current Standing</u>

Language Arts - B

Math - C

Social Studies - A

Science - C

Elective - B

F. Goals

The second section of the goal chart is where your students will actually set their goals. Their goals answer the question, "Where am I going?" As stated previously, this is where your students will write concrete, attainable goals. These are the targets that your students are aiming for.

Beneath the current standing section of the goal chart, have your students write the subheading, - Goals, and beneath that, they should list each of their subjects and write the grades (goals) they expect to achieve beside them. On the following page is a sample outline of the current standing and goal sections of the goal chart.

BARUTI'S GOALS

Marking Period #2

<u>Current Standing</u>	<u>Goals</u>
Language Arts - B	**Language Arts - A**
Math - C	**Math - B**
Social Studies - A	**Social Studies - A**
Science - C	**Science - B**
Elective - B	**Elective - A**

G. Strategy

The next section of the goal chart is where your students will develop their strategy or plan of action. It answers the question, "How am I going to get there?" This is probably the most difficult part of goal setting because this is where the actual work comes in to play. In other words, anybody can *say* that they are going to achieve a particular goal, but the true test is developing a detailed plan towards achieving your goals and then consistently adhering to your plan.

I find it amazing how so many people will set particular goals for themselves, but do not see the significance in devising a strategy. When you look at sports for example, you see that there is far more planning than actual playing. For instance, professional football has four 15 minute quarters. This totals exactly 60 minutes of playing time. The average game is on television however for about three hours. This is because after each play, the teams go into a huddle to formulate a strategy for the very next play. They do this for the entire game. Additionally, during half-time they plan and during the entire week, the teams plan. If all of this planning takes place during a football game and throughout the week, it certainly makes sense that a wealth of planning should go into achieving academic excellence in the classroom as well.

Your students' plan provides them with organization towards achieving their goals. It enables them to know exactly what it is that they need to do in order to experience success.

Returning to the goal chart, beneath the goals section, have your students write the subheading - Strategy, and beneath that, list each subject and write a detailed plan for achieving the marking period grade (goal) that was set for each. For example, a generic strategy for a particular subject area might state:

A. <u>In Class</u>
   • I will always come to class prepared.
   • I will always pay attention in class.
   • I will always take good class notes.
   • I will always ask questions whenever necessary.
   • I will always complete my assignments and submit on time.

B. <u>At Home</u>
   • I will always begin my homework upon arrival home from school.
   • I will always keep the television and music off during homework and study time.
   • I will always work in an environment that is organized, tidy and well lit.
   • I will always complete my homework assignments and review with my parent(s).
   • I will always study every subject for a minimum of thirty minutes each and quiz myself.

On the following page is a completed sample outline of the goal chart.

BARUTI'S GOALS

Marking Period #2

Current Standing	Goals
Language Arts - B	Language Arts - A
Math - C	Math - B
Social Studies - A	Social Studies - A
Science - C	Science - B
Elective - B	Elective - A

Strategy

Language Arts -

Math -

Social Studies -

Science -

Elective -

If you teach in a departmentalized setting and therefore teach only one or two subjects, you would follow the same format, but with the subject area(s) you teach only. I would therefore recommend that you use index cards which I refer to as "goal cards" instead of full sheets of paper since you are servicing more students than teachers of self-contained classrooms. Teachers that teach one subject area may see upwards of 125 students per day. The index cards will therefore consume less wall space than full sheets of paper.

After your students have completed their goal charts or goal cards, they should be posted on the wall in some visible area of your classroom to allow your students to review on a daily basis. You should regularly challenge your students to work hard and consistently towards achieving their goals. Reviewing their goals regularly will enable both you and your students to continually evaluate their progress. If your students deviate from their goals and strategies, you will be in a better position to steer them back on track because their marking period goals and strategies are written and posted.

At the end of each marking period, your students should compare their goals with the actual grades received. For those subject areas in which your students either met or exceeded their goals, they are now ready to set higher goals for the next marking period's goal chart. For those subject areas in which your students did not reach their goals, you must collectively determine what it was that prevented them from experiencing success. They should review the strategy section of their goal chart to determine whether or not they did everything that they wrote they would do to achieve the goals set. In planning for the next marking period's goal chart, be sure to encourage your students to make whatever adjustments are needed to be made in their strategy. For any subject area that the goal was not achieved, the same goal should be set in the new marking period, but again with a revised strategy. This should provide your students with even more motivation to be successful the next time around.

"Wall of Fame"

If your students are going to experience academic success, they must be inspired to achieve academic success. If they are not inspired to achieve, chances are good that they will not succeed. Referring to the achievement gap between African American and white students, African American students deserve to be in learning environments that are inspirational and conducive to achieving academic excellence.

In developing a classroom environment that is inspirational and conducive to achieving academic excellence, it is of paramount importance that the environment is one that recognizes and celebrates progress and achievement. One way of doing this is to develop a "Wall of Fame" that is designated for student achievement. Although a particular wall may be labeled as a wall of fame, you can personalize it as I did in my classroom as "The Mind Zone Wall of Fame." This gives your students more of a sense of ownership of "their" wall of fame. There are a variety of different things that could be displayed on your wall of fame. Following are a few suggestions.

A. Students of the Month Recognition

As students perform to your expectations in your classroom, they need frequent recognition and reinforcement in an effort to keep them excited about achievement over a period of time. One strategy for keeping your students inspired is to recognize students of the month. In your attempts of recognizing as many students in your class as possible, you wouldn't want a student of the month model that recognizes your top students only. You'll want a model that will enable all students the opportunity for recognition. Your students will therefore be competing not against one another, but they will be competing against a criteria. In other words, in developing your students of the month model, you should devise a criteria that all of your students will be held accountable for meeting such as the following:

- A's and/or B's on all tests and quizzes
- A's and/or B's on all classroom projects
- All homework assignments fully completed
- Excellent classroom behavior
- Excellent classroom participation

Of course, your student of the month model may vary from the one above based upon the needs of the students in your classroom. You will need to assess where your students currently stand towards meeting the above criteria and make whatever adjustments you deem to be appropriate for your students to be successful.

In order to recognize your students of the month, you could make small or large certificates on a computer (depending upon the number of students that meet the criteria and the amount of available wall space in your classroom) and have a short ceremony each month as you post the certificates on your wall of fame. You should make two copies of each certificate so that the students can also take a copy home to be posted in their bedrooms. Your students of the month recognition should take place on the first day of the following month. Trust me; your students will be looking forward to it and you will feel equally excited about their accomplishments.

B. Homework Award Recognition

A second classroom achievement recognition incentive is to recognize students for completing all homework assignments during the month as you did with your students of the month. Your criteria could be simply to complete all homework assignments while adhering to your homework policy (to be discussed in Chapter Six - Managing Your Classroom).

As with the student of the month recognition, your homework award recognition should take place on the first day of the following month through the posting of certificates on your wall of fame. You should also present certificates for your students to take home.

C. Perfect Attendance Recognition

In some cases, performance is low simply because attendance is poor. In an effort to improve attendance, you should recognize and celebrate perfect attendance each Monday morning for the previous week You wouldn't need to have a formal ceremony but you may want to type up a list of all students that had perfect attendance and post the list on your wall of fame. Once on the list, many students will want to remain on the list and therefore report to school every day, all year long.

D. Honor Roll Recognition

In most schools, there is a quarterly achievement recognition assembly that acknowledges all students that achieved academic distinction. In addition to the school level assembly, you could have your own classroom quarterly program where you recognize your students who achieved academic distinction and post their certificates on the wall of fame. This personalizes the quarterly achievement recognition and allows you the opportunity to use the ceremony as a platform to encourage the other students to strive for excellence as well.

E. Student Work Samples

Student work samples should always be posted on your wall of fame or hall walls for everyone to see. Students feel good about themselves when they perform well and therefore have the opportunity of seeing their work posted on the wall. Posting student work on the wall also sends the message to your students that you value their achievement.

In your displaying of your students' work samples, be sure to keep only current work on the walls. I would suggest that at the end of every month, your students' work samples be replaced with more current work, with the exception of those assignments that were posted towards the end of a given month.

Classroom Competitions

There are a variety of classroom competitions you can conduct with your students in an effort to keep them inspired and motivated such as public speaking competitions, essay writing competitions, subject area competitions and spelling bees. These competitions can be on an individual basis or a team basis. Classroom competitions have the potential of making learning fun due to the competitive nature of the competitions and the desire to win. This can potentially motivate your students to put forth their best effort towards winning while simultaneously forcing them to put forth their best effort towards preparing.

Teaching With Optimism

In your role of classroom teacher, you are the leader in the classroom. In your capacity as both teacher and leader, you must possess a high level of optimism towards your students' success. If you have doubts regarding their ability to become successful in your classroom, your doubts will be conveyed to your students through your attitude, speech and behavior towards them. Once they have construed that you lack confidence in their ability to achieve success, your own ability to keep them inspired becomes inhibited. Despite whatever odds, challenges or obstacles you and your students may encounter, as the classroom teacher of African American students who are on the low end of the achievement gap, you must maintain a high level of optimism towards your students' abilities to achieve academic excellence at all times.

Imagine entering the classroom everyday with the notion that your students are failures and cannot achieve academic excellence. With this attitude, unless your entire class is self-motivated, they are doomed to failure because the teacher and therefore the leader of the classroom has made it clear to his students through his attitude, speech and behavior that he does not believe in their ability to achieve success. As a tactic for inspiring your students, you must enter your classroom each and every day with the attitude that your students will in fact achieve academic excellence.

Teaching With Energy, Enthusiasm and Passion

Have you ever had to sit through a year of school or a class in college with a teacher or professor that bored you to no end? Chances are that you disliked attending this class and that you did not perform as well as you would have if you had a teacher with a high level of energy, enthusiasm and passion for what was being taught and who was being taught. If you did have a teacher like this and you did in fact struggle with having to attend the class, imagine what it must be like for your students if you are boring and unenthusiastic.

In an effort to keep your students inspired, you must approach your lessons with a high level of energy, enthusiasm and passion for what you teach and who you teach. When your students discern anything less, your chances of being able to hold their attention and to keep them inspired diminishes. Your energy, enthusiasm and passion for what you do as a classroom teacher increases your chances of making learning fun, stimulating and engaging for your students.

Unequivocal Commitment to Student Achievement

Towards inspiring your students to achieve academic excellence, you must exhibit an unequivocal commitment to student achievement which includes maintaining high academic standards and expectations for all of the students you teach. Everything that you do in your planning and preparation, and everything that you do in your classroom must convey your commitment to your students' overall achievement. Without an unequivocal commitment to your students' success, they are in turn being shortchanged by a teacher who is not committed to giving his all. The consequence becomes less than optimal achievement of the students being serviced. In raising the achievement levels of African American students, an unequivocal commitment to their educational growth and development must be the standard of the teacher.

4. EFFECTIVE CLASSROOM INSTRUCTION

As a classroom teacher, the main thing that you do is teach students. Your primary role is to provide quality instruction to your students on a daily basis. Everything discussed in the previous three chapters is all for naught if you lack effectiveness in your daily instruction. Additionally, as an effective classroom teacher, it is unavoidable that you have an expertise in the content area(s) you teach.

Content Area Expertise

As a teacher of African American children, it is unavoidable and inexcusable to have anything less than an expertise in the content area(s) you teach. You cannot be effective with what you do not know. When attempts are made by teachers to teach what they do not know or have little familiarity with, the students are the ones that ultimately suffer. With current achievement levels being where they are, African American students deserve to have classroom teachers that have an expertise in the subject areas being taught. More specifically, African American students deserve to have teachers who are highly qualified and capable of teaching the required curriculum.

African American standardized math scores continue to be alarmingly low throughout the U.S.; particularly at the 8th grade level. There are certainly many causes for the low achievement African American students have been experiencing on standardized assessments in math, in which I have examined several in the previous chapters. One could certainly make the argument that teachers of both 7th and 8th grade math must be math certified as opposed to elementary certified. Presently at the middle school level, the certification that is required to teach middle school in most states is an elementary certification. As of the time of this writing, under the federal No Child Left Behind legislation, this seems to be changing, but in the interim, the reality is that 7th and 8th grade African American students are subjected to in large part, teachers of elementary certifications where at the 7th and 8th grade levels, secondary certifications are required and desired.

It should be common sense to most that if students are going to achieve academic excellence, their teachers must have an expertise in what they teach. If I am a teacher of math, I must have an expertise in math. If I am a teacher of reading, I must have an expertise in teaching reading. In fact, I should be a reading specialist. If I am a teacher of science, I must have an expertise in all of the areas of science I am assigned to teach. If I am a teacher of social studies, I must have an expertise in the areas of social studies or history I am assigned to teach. Anything less will deprive the students of what the district curriculum and state standards require for learning, assessing and eventually graduating.

Imagine that a non musician is assigned to teach an advanced violin class, for example. More than likely, it will never happen. There is absolutely no way that a non musician can teach an instrumental music class for playing any instrument. In fact, we wouldn't expect this to occur. But in the core content areas of math, language arts, science or social studies, we may see almost anyone with an elementary certification teaching any of these subjects between grades K - 8 and then wonder why the students are not achieving.

As an urban public school educator for the past fifteen years, I can certainly understand why some teachers are assigned to teach outside of their areas of expertise. There continues to be a very serious shortage of qualified teachers; particularly in the areas of math and science in urban public school districts at the middle and high school levels. With the reality of a shortage of teachers, school districts are forced to fill vacancies with whomever is available with the intention of providing them with adequate professional development. But again, the losers are invariably African American students who must endure teachers who in many cases are underqualified to teach them at the middle and high school levels.

If you meet the above criteria as a teacher of African American students, I urge you to engage in as much professional development as you can relative to developing your expertise in the content area(s) you teach.

Introducing and Concluding Your Lessons

Whatever instructional approach or model you implement in your classroom, no model will be effective if you are unsuccessful in gaining the attention of your students. Once you are ready to teach, you must have your students' attention. Attempting to start your lesson without having gained the attention of your students is tantamount to coming to school and telling your students that they can have the day to themselves, because as long as you are teaching without their attention, that is essentially what they will have.

When I was a classroom teacher, I always greeted my students in the hallway and briefed them on my expectations for the period. They then went into the classroom and worked on the "do now" of the day. When I felt they were ready, I stood in the front of the classroom and said to my students, HOTEP! They responded back in unison, HOTEP! Hotep is an ancient Egyptian greeting meaning peace. I had disciplined my students to know that once I said Hotep, we were ready to begin. In other words, Hotep was my attention grabber. You must have a strategy that enables you to gain your students' attention prior to starting your lessons. It may be something as simple as using a key word as I did.

Once you have completed all preliminary duties and have gained the attention of your students, you are now ready to introduce your lesson. Your lesson should always open with some kind of a lead-in that prepares students for learning. You may want to recap something that was covered the previous day that ties in to the current lesson or you may want to open with something that is not necessarily related to the previous day, but serves as a good introduction for the skill or concept being taught today. In other words, you want to open with something that connects to your students' prior knowledge in an effort to draw them in to the new lesson while simultaneously holding their attention.

After the introduction which should take no more than 2 - 3 minutes, you should state the current lesson objective, which should have already been written prominently on your board. Your lesson objective should be expressed behaviorally using a verb, as its purpose is to tell your students what you expect them to be able to accomplish by the end of the lesson, ie. "By the end of the lesson, students will be able to distinguish between the philosophies of W. E. B. DuBois and Booker T. Washington." Your lesson objective should always be stated by you before teaching the lesson. It should also be stated by one or two students for reinforcement. It is imperative that while you are teaching your lesson, all of your students are aware of the lesson objective.

At the conclusion of the lesson, you'll want to be sure to bring your lesson to closure. Bringing your lesson to closure may be as simple as asking two or three students to summarize what they learned today to reinforce what was covered, or you might have a student or two to restate something that was learned. Be sure to always allow yourself enough time to close your lessons as opposed to getting to the end of the period and abruptly stopping your lesson until the next day. Your closure enables you to reinforce a specific skill or concept that was covered during the lesson.

Teacher-centered versus Student-centered Instruction

During your lessons, who does all or most of the talking? Is it you or is it your students? In a teacher-centered classroom, it is the teacher who does most or all of the talking. The students sit there for entire periods or blocks listening (hopefully) to the teacher teach the lesson of the day. As I often say, the teacher winds up being the star of the show with a less than enthusiastic audience to speak to. In a student-centered classroom, the teacher's talking is minimal. The teacher engages the students in doing the talking by way of working collaboratively in cooperative learning groups solving various assigned problems. The students therefore become the stars of the show.

As a grade school and high school student, I can still remember virtually all of my teachers and my experiences in their classrooms. I cannot say that I have any fond memories of any particular teachers or classes where learning was actually fun, stimulating and engaging. My recollection of being a student in school is a teacher standing in front of the classroom lecturing for long periods of time. I recall not being particularly interested in school because the experience for me was rather boring. Everyday, it was the same routine - come to school, listen to the teacher all day and then go home. Again, nothing fun; nothing stimulating; nothing engaging about learning.

As an adult and an educator, I've thought about this numerous times over the years with the hope that I would not be guilty of repeating the same practice as a teacher nor accepting of it from my staff as a principal.

In order for students to genuinely want to come to school and learn for 180 days, classroom instruction and therefore learning has got to be fun, stimulating and engaging. You have to be willing to relinquish your "stardom" if you haven't done so already, so that the attention can be devoted to engaging your students. Your students must be given the opportunity to work and learn collaboratively within a cooperative learning format. Cooperative learning has the potential of making learning fun, stimulating and engaging. When you have the ability to make learning fun, stimulating and engaging, the probability for your students achieving academic excellence increases.

Oftentimes, I here teachers make the contention that they do not engage students in cooperative lessons because they feel that their students lack the social skills to be productive. They contend that through poor social skills, the lessons are loud and disorderly. My response is that if poor student social skills are in fact a deterrent to productive cooperative learning, it is then incumbent upon the teacher to teach social skills development. The teaching of social skills may involve you modeling expected and undesirable behaviors in a role playing exercise with another student in front of the classroom, which would be followed up with a class discussion of what was observed. This could then expand to students being engaged in social skills lessons that involve pairs of students. As students demonstrate progress in working in pairs, the groups can be expanded to three and four students with the focus not being on content area lessons, but on social skills development. As students continue to make progress in developing their social skills, they will be better prepared to engage in cooperative learning lessons.

Another contention I hear from teachers as to why they do not engage their students in cooperative learning lessons is that they have too much content that they need to cover or that their students' knowledge base is so deficient that they need to spend entire periods or blocks engaged in direct instruction. Again, I couldn't disagree more. All of what needs to be taught can be covered in cooperative learning groups, with you providing the initial mini-lesson before engaging your students in the cooperative learning lesson.

The key in making the transition from teacher-centered instruction to a student-centered instructional approach through cooperative learning is the willingness of the teacher to relinquish "stardom" and allowing the students to shine.

Differentiating Your Instruction

A typical classroom is comprised of anywhere from 20 - 25 students. Of course, there are school districts that have been able to keep their class sizes below 18 students just as there are school districts with class sizes in excess of 35 students. For our purposes however, a typical class size of 20 students for example, potentially has 20 different learning styles. This means that in classrooms throughout the U.S where the teachers' preferred instructional approach is a teacher-centered approach; unless all of the students in the classroom are auditory learners, not a great deal of actual learning is taking place. Teacher-centered instruction via a lecture will address the needs of some of your students - the ones who are auditory learners. All others will invariably struggle.

It is your responsibility to thoroughly familiarize yourself with the learning styles of all of your students. If you are going to be successful as their teacher, you must know how they learn, while making the valid assumption that they do not all learn alike. Some of your students are auditory learners, some are visual learners, some learn better in cooperative settings, some are left-brain learners while others are right-brain learners. As a resource, I strongly recommend you read the various literature and research on multiple intelligences, constructivist learning and differentiating instruction.

Once you have determined the learning styles of the learners in your classroom, you must determine how you will address them. You will have to differentiate or personalize your instruction so that all of the students in your classroom have an equal opportunity for success.

In integrated schools and school districts where there is a combination of African American and white students, you find that based on available data, the African American students score as an aggregate far below the white students. This begs the logical question; are the teachers adequately addressing the learning styles of their African American students? In other words, questions need to be sufficiently answered relative to the disparity in achievement between African American and white students.

Frequently, once we get into the flow of a school year and certain students emerge as the high achievers of the class, assumptions begin to be made that these are the brighter students. This may or may not be the case however. One must also take into consideration that perhaps these students are achieving because their particular learning styles are being addressed according to the preferred instructional approach of the teacher. Differentiating your instruction allows you to teach to the learning styles of the different learners in your classroom. This way, all students have an equal opportunity for success.

Obviously, this will require a great deal of time, effort and planning on your part as the teacher. It is very easy to come to school every day and engage your students in lectures throughout the day. It is quite another thing to get to know your students, become familiar with their learning styles, develop lesson plans that address their learning styles and then implement differentiated instruction. The students who stand the greatest chance for success will be the ones whose teachers are thoroughly prepared to teach them.

Interdisciplinary Instruction

Towards raising the achievement levels of your African American students, teachers require a huge repertoire of instructional and motivation approaches for success. Another instructional approach which should either be utilized within self-contained classrooms or between departmentalized classrooms is interdisciplinary instruction. Interdisciplinary instruction allows teachers to take individual concepts and make them real across content areas and thereby increasing the probability that comprehension will occur. Interdisciplinary instruction also enables students to see the interrelationship of all their individual subject areas.

In a study of the life of the African American inventor, astronomer and mathematician, Benjamin Banneker for example, interdisciplinary instruction would be very appropriate. In the study of Banneker's life, there are implications for math, science, language arts and social studies instruction. The relevance of Banneker's life becomes much more meaningful when students are given the opportunity to grasp the fullness of it across all the content areas.

As a self-contained classroom teacher utilizing interdisciplinary instruction, the planning of your lessons will require identifying themes that span across all of the subject areas you teach. As a subject area teacher utilizing interdisciplinary instruction, you will be required to plan collaboratively with the other teachers of your students towards developing interdisciplinary lessons.

As with differentiated instruction, interdisciplinary planning and instruction will require a great deal of time and effort. Teachers that teach their subjects in isolation actually do their subjects and their students a great disservice by engaging in this outdated instructional practice. Although interdisciplinary instruction is not a new concept, it remains to be an underutilized means of teaching. In your efforts of raising the achievement levels of African American students, it is imperative that all research-based instructional models be utilized in your classrooms.

Brain-based Instruction

In all of the conversations, discussions and debates I have had over the years regarding the problems associated with effectively educating African American children, and the various conferences, workshops, panel discussions and lectures I have attended regarding the same, seldom is the topic of brain-based instruction ever addressed or considered as a serious topic of discussion. I find this to be rather peculiar considering that it is the brain that processes and makes sense out of information as it is perceived through the senses.

There is a wealth of available information on brain theory, brain-based instruction and brain-based classrooms. As the debate continues regarding how best to educate African American children, educators must become more knowledgeable about the role of the brain.

Over the years in my readings of the functioning of the brain, I have come across arguments for certain ethnic groups favoring one hemisphere of the brain over the other and the relationship between culture and favoring one hemisphere of the brain over the other. I won't elaborate here because the research findings are still inconclusive. I mention it solely to encourage you to investigate further the workings of the brain and how it impacts on the instruction of African American children. In other words, as teachers, you need to be familiar with the implications of your instructional practices relative to their impact on how the brain processes information. Furthermore, if in fact, different cultures favor one hemisphere of the brain over the other with the left hemisphere being more analytical and the right hemisphere being more synthesizing, there is a need to ensure that you are teaching to the appropriate side of the brain in your classroom. This will therefore require that you incorporate the study of the brain with your other professional reading and overall professional development.

Child Development Research

In addition to becoming knowledgeable of the brain and how it processes information, you need to be knowledgeable of the current research in child development. In developing a familiarity with the students you teach, a part of your familiarity is understanding how they develop socially and emotionally. As you gain an understanding of the social-emotional development of your students, you are in a better position to understand the social-emotional changes that your students are experiencing through the maturation process and its inherent impact on learning. If you are going to make the kinds of connections with your students that will increase the probability that they are going to achieve academic excellence, the study of child development research is essential.

5. PLANNING AND ORGANIZATION

Planning and organization are at the very core of what you do in your overall practice as a classroom teacher. Without proper and regular planning, you are teaching with little if any focus or direction. Without organization, you lack a system or routine for what you do. Your teaching is consequently haphazard at best. Everything you do as a classroom teacher requires a tremendous amount of planning and organization towards effective implementation. Your overall effectiveness will be determined in part by how well you plan and how organized you are in your planning efforts. If you *fail* to *plan*, you are essentially *planning* to *fail*. When you *plan* your *work*, you are essentially preparing to *work* your *plan*.

Planning for the New School Year

Planning is actually an ongoing effort. For the start of each school year, it begins in the summer (after you have taken time off to regroup from a long and productive previous school year). After you have regrouped, your planning for the forthcoming school year must commence before it is time for you to report back to work.

A. Self-Reflecting and Self-Assessing Revisited

Before the start of a new school year, you must devote time to reflecting and assessing. Similar to the daily self-reflection and self-assessment referred to in Chapter Two, you should reflect upon and assess the past school year. Beginning with the start of the preceding school year, try to recall as much of it as you can without making judgment. Simply reflect. After you have concluded your self-reflection, proceed to your self-assessment. Think about what strategies worked well and why. Also think about what strategies were ineffective and why. As you are reflecting and assessing, be sure to refer to your reflection journal from the previous school year.

B. Reassessment of Purpose, Mission and Vision

After reflecting and assessing, you will need to reassess your purpose for teaching, your mission and your vision. You'll need to assess whether or not your performance of the previous school year was consistent with your purpose, mission and vision. You may also need to redefine your purpose, mission and vision. Whether they have remained the same or you will be making adjustments for the new school year, in a new reflection journal, you will need to write your purpose for teaching, your mission for the forthcoming school year and your overall vision for yourself as the teacher, and your students' performance over the course of the year. Also be sure to examine last year's incremental goals and make adjustments wherever you deem necessary.

C. Assessment of Student Achievement

After reassessing your purpose, mission and vision, you'll want to review your students' overall academic performance in the subject areas you teach from the preceding school year. Review the overall grade distribution of your students and determine why the grades resulted in the grades that were achieved. You will then want to devise a plan for improvement for the forthcoming school year. In devising your plan, you should also set new grade distribution goals relative to the number and percentage of students who will receive A's and B's over the course of the school year. Your grade distribution goals would be considered an increment of the incremental goals discussed in Chapter Two relative to fulfilling your overall vision.

In planning for improvement in student achievement, you should also consider your past effectiveness in areas such as keeping your students motivated, your content area expertise, your instructional approach, taking advantage of professional development opportunities and how you engage your students' parents.

D. Review of District Curriculum and State Standards

After assessing student performance, you will need to review your district curriculum and your state's content standards. It is very difficult for you to teach at an optimal level if you are not fully knowledgeable of your district's curriculum and your state's content standards. These two documents lay the foundation for your daily instruction. They drive your instruction on a daily basis. In raising the achievement levels of African American students, it should be only under rare circumstances that your instruction deviates from the curriculum and standards. Although one could certainly make the argument for quality instruction that goes beyond the curriculum and standards, the reality is that student, school and school district performance is measured by how well students perform on standardized assessments. As teachers of African American students, you then have no choice but to teach to your district's curriculum and your state's standards on a daily and consistent basis.

Inherent in your review of the curriculum and standards are your state's test specifications. If students and all other stake holders are being held accountable for student performance on standardized assessments, it will be expedient that you also review, familiarize and become knowledgeable of your state's standardized test specifications. In other words, you and your students must have familiarity with the tests that will be administered which increases the probability for improved student performance. Without knowledge of the test-specifications, you lack a basis for preparing lessons that address improved student performance. When on the other hand, you are armed with an understanding of what the test is comprised of, you are in a better position to expose your students to lessons which enhance student performance.

E. Assessment of Classroom Management

After reviewing your curriculum and standards, you will need to assess your classroom management procedures. If you found them to be effective relative to both student behavior and student performance, you should plan to retain them for the forthcoming school year. If on the other hand you have determined that they were less than optimal, you should at this time make the adjustments that need to be made in order for you to be able to maximize student time on task.

Planning Throughout the School Year

Once you get into the regular routine of the school year, you will need to plan on an ongoing basis. As stated previously, planning is at the foundation of what you do as a teacher. Without proper planning, you have no direction nor focus for your daily instruction.

Each week, you are required to write and submit your daily lesson plans for the forthcoming week to your evaluator of record. Some principals prefer them on Friday afternoons while other principals prefer them on Monday mornings. Monday morning submissions enable teachers to have the entire weekend to work on lesson planning.

In developing your lesson plans, as stated in the previous section, you must utilize your district curriculum and your state's content standards. Collectively, they must drive your weekly lesson planning and your daily instruction.

Inherent in your lesson plan development should be the utilization of achievement data to plan your lessons. Your students' achievement data provides you with an analysis of what kind of progress your students are making under your tutelage. Minimally, on a weekly basis as you are developing your lesson plans, you should analyze your students' grades and identify patterns in achievement and/or failure. You should examine all of the progress indicators that you normally utilize which include standardized assessment data. As you develop your lesson plans, this data should form the basis for how you sequence your lessons and how you differentiate your instruction. As stated in Chapter Four, you have several different learning styles in your classroom and not all students are achieving and advancing at the same rate. Your achievement data should therefore drive your decision-making regarding how you plan your lessons for all of the students in your classroom.

Remember that the reality of the achievement gap between African American and white students is in your hands. In other words, your effectiveness as the classroom teacher will determine whether or not the achievement gap is widened or shortened. Your planning must therefore effectively address the learning needs of all of your students if meaningful progress is going to be made in your classroom.

Organizing for Results

In addition to thorough and thoughtful planning, as a classroom teacher, you must also be highly organized. Your ability to organize yourself will positively impact your overall practice as a teacher. The ability to balance teaching 20 - 25 or more students within one classroom is a challenge in and of itself. Taking into consideration the various learning, social and emotional needs of your students, it is most crucial that you have superior organizational skills. Following, I will highlight some areas where you should be particularly organized if you are going to experience success as a classroom teacher.

A. Grade Register

An organized grade register is a must for a classroom teacher. First and foremost, you must develop a habit of grading papers upon receipt and immediately recording the grades in your grade register. Anything less will result in your falling behind while accumulating stacks of ungraded papers which are not accounted for in your grade register. At any time that your students' parents request to see their children's grades, you should have all of your students' grades recorded in your grade register so that all grades are accounted for and can be reviewed.

In organizing your grade register, there are a variety of formats which may be utilized. There are several software packages available that virtually do everything for you. I think that these are the best choice. All of your calculations are done for you and your entire grade register can be organized by category.

If you choose to use a manual system, you can still maintain the same results as the software system, but you will be required to do more work. You will have to develop a system that is easy for you to explain and defend to your students' parents and your building administrators.

In setting up your grading system, you will need to determine a grading system that addresses the various grades that you assign such as tests, quizzes, homework assignments and projects. You will also need to determine what percentage of the overall report card grade each will receive. Whatever system and format you use however, be certain that you are able to adequately explain it and defend it.

B. Class Work and Homework Policy

Your class work and homework policy also speaks to your level of organization. You must develop a class work and homework policy that your students will be held accountable for complying with. They must understand that all work is expected to be completed within the guidelines of the policy which includes meeting your submission deadline. Anything less would be considered unacceptable. In holding your students accountable for compliance with your class work and homework policy, your students are learning the principles of responsibility and accountability. Towards developing your policy, you may want to consider provisions such as:

- Writing on the front side of the paper first
- Black or dark blue ink only (except for math)
- Cursive handwriting on all non-math assignments
- Proper heading
- No folded work
- No wrinkled work
- No torn work
- No smudges or smears
- Minimal grammatical errors relative to the following:
  a. spelling
  b. capitalization
  c. punctuation
  d. indentation
  e. usage of margins

What the above policy really boils down to is neatness and organization. It is inevitable that there will be students who feel that a policy such as this is too stringent. You must remind your students that their work is a reflection of who they are and that they will therefore be held accountable for the submission of quality work on a regular basis.

C. Student Folders

It is unavoidable that you have student work folders for all of your students. The best way to organize is to have a separate folder for each subject area that you teach. Contained in each folder will be work samples, teacher-generated assessments and standardized assessments. All student work should be dated and ordered sequentially with the most recent work on top. There should be a representative amount of work contained in all folders. All work samples should also be graded. If you are a Language Arts teacher, you should have a separate folder for student writing samples. All writing samples should also be scored, dated and ordered sequentially.

In my previous discussion of utilizing data to plan lessons, the work accumulated and contained in your student folders is another source of data. Your students' folders serve as a record of progress made over a period of time. This is why it is so important that all work is dated and ordered sequentially. By reviewing your students' folders, you are better able to monitor student progress.

Towards raising the achievement levels of your African American students, you as the teacher must be very knowledgeable of your students' academic strengths and weaknesses. By organizing your students' work into folders, you are in a much better position to study, review, monitor and analyze all accumulated work collected.

D. Grading Papers and Returning to Students

Whenever you are preparing your students for a test, it is good practice to tell your students in advance when the test will be administered. You'd then spend the days leading up to the test getting your students prepared and on test day, administer the test. If you were effective towards preparing and motivating your students for this assessment, they were then prepared and eager to get it over with. After completion of the test, it is only natural then that the students will want their results back as quickly as possible. This is where your organizational skill comes in. If you have an expectation for your students to be prepared on your predetermined dates, it is your responsibility to get their tests and other submissions back to them in a timely fashion. When I was a classroom teacher, regardless of the quantity of work to be graded, I always made it my business to get my students' work back to them by the next school day. This required that I organized my schedule so that on days that I had a lot of grading to do, I had very few other responsibilities on that particular day or evening.

You too must organize yourself and your schedule so that your students' work can be returned to them as quickly as possible. This in turn shows them that you have a strong interest in their work performance because they see that you took the time to grade their work immediately following submission.

E. Maintaining Records

As a classroom teacher, there are various records that you must maintain relative to your being organized such as discipline records and parent contact information.

Discipline Records

Whenever a student has to be disciplined either by you or a colleague, you must maintain a record of the infraction including how the infraction was dealt with. You should prepare a discipline file for each of your students so that whenever they engage in undesirable behaviors, you can insert your documentation into their personal discipline folders. This way, when you meet with or notify parents, you have a record of all infractions committed.

Parent Contact Information

Typically, in urban communities, student phone numbers and addresses change often. Resultantly, it is imperative that you maintain an active parent contact file. You must always be able to contact either a parent or a relative. Your students should be regularly encouraged to inform you of any changes that may occur in their parent contact information. This file should also contain a parent contact log for all parent contacts made and attempted.

F. Classroom Layout

In setting up your classroom, there must be a rationale relative to how you have organized your room. The decision to arrange your students' desks into clusters or rows for example speaks to how you organize your classroom and therefore organize learning. Other classroom layout decisions such as where to place the classroom library, the location of the classroom learning center and classroom computers again speak to not only how you organize learning, but also to your own organizational skill.

I have visited many classrooms where it was more than obvious that no thought at all went into the organization of the classroom. Various items were situated where they were at random. It was apparent that little if any thought went into why the classroom was arranged the way that it was.

As a classroom teacher of African American children, you must consciously organize the layout of your classroom in a way that increases the probability for optimal learning to occur. The layout of your classroom is essentially the learning environment you have created for your students which will in part determine the success level of your students.

G. Usage of Chalkboard and Overhead Projector

How you utilize your chalkboard and/or overhead projector speaks to your level of organization. Let's look at both separately.

Chalkboard

Using the chalkboard is not simply going to the board and writing on it during classroom instruction. The bulk of what goes on your chalkboard should be written before your students even enter the classroom for the day. Each minute of your teaching time is far too valuable for you to have to stop instruction to write on or develop your chalkboard.

If you are a self-contained teacher with a large amount of board space, it is recommended that you devote portions of the board for each of the subject areas you teach. You must then write all pertinent information on the board before your students enter the classroom, which includes the writing of your lesson objectives.

The best time to prepare your boards is after school so that they are ready for use the next school day. You must be sure to clean them first. Your children need to be able to see and read from boards that are not obscured by erased chalk. The ability to consistently prepare your chalkboards before your students enter the room speaks to your level of organization for effective instruction.

Overhead Projector

Overhead projectors are ideal for displaying information because the number of transparencies that can be prepared is limitless. While writing your weekly lesson plans, you can develop transparencies that coincide with each individual lesson. You therefore do not need to be concerned about erasing the chalkboard and writing new information in the middle of instruction. All you have to do is simply change the transparency. The usage of transparencies is then a very effective way to prevent losing valuable instructional time that is often lost through using chalkboards.

H. Time Management

In being highly organized, good usage of time is an absolute must. From the time that you enter the building until the time that you leave, how you use and manage your time is critical to your overall effectiveness. Whether you are a self-contained teacher or a subject area teacher, you only have a limited amount of time to teach each subject or class. Your planning must therefore be such that you have organized your entire day and know what it is that will be covered throughout each instructional period. It is a given that adjustments will need to be made once you are into your actual teaching but your organization at least provides you with a framework for proceeding forward.

You must also be able to manage your time for the times when your students are not in school. Grading student work for example, can be quite time consuming. You must organize your time and schedule so that your grading can be completed daily, yet not imposing on all of your afternoon and evening time. You must also make time for yourself which includes rest so that you will be well rested for each succeeding day.

I. Teacher Filing System

Just as you need to maintain student folders for all of your students, you also need to maintain a good filing system for yourself. There are various documents that you will receive from your administration that you may need to make reference to at some later date. Every document that you receive from your administration should go into your file. There are also various other documents that will emanate from your overall practice of teaching such as your classroom management plan, procedures for various activities you engage your students in, discipline records, parent contact information or notes from parents. In being organized, you must develop a filing system that is alphabetized and will enable you to put your hands on any and all documents you accumulated over the course of either your career or your tenure in a particular building.

Again, planning and organization are essential to your practice as a classroom teacher. Always spend sufficient time planning and organizing which increases the probability that your students will enjoy success in your classroom.

Student Planners and Notebooks

Just as you must be organized, you must also ensure that your students are organized. At the core of their organization is obtaining and maintaining student planners and notebooks.

A. Student Planners

As your students' teacher, you are going to hold them accountable for a variety of different tasks including class work and homework assignments, tests and quizzes, individual and group projects, book reports and research papers. In order for your students to adequately prepare and stay organized, they will need to record all of your assignments, test dates and due dates in their planners. You must therefore require that all of your students obtain a planner and that they bring it to class along with their other books, materials and supplies everyday. They must also be required to record all pertinent information in their planners in a timely fashion. Be sure to remind your students' parents to review their children's planners on a nightly basis and verify their review by providing their signature.

B. Notebooks

In order to increase the probability that what is learned each day is retained, your students must have a notebook for each of their subject areas. They must then be required to take good notes that they will be able to study from on a nightly basis. Never assume that your students are already skilled at taking good notes. Note-taking is a skill which will have to be taught. You must therefore devote time to teaching your students how best to organize their notebooks and how to take good notes so that studying their notes is both purposeful and beneficial.

6.   MANAGING YOUR CLASSROOM

A few years back when I was a classroom teacher, I worked next door to a new teacher who was fresh out of college. She was a 6th grade language arts teacher. When it came to content knowledge, she was second to none. She absolutely knew her content area. Additionally, she had a sense of purpose, she was on a mission and she had a definite vision for her students' success over the course of the school year. She was also highly motivated and came to school each and every day ready to inspire her students to reach new heights. But despite her content area expertise and mindset which was geared for success, her first year of teaching turned out to be rather stressful for her. Why? Because she had not mastered the art of managing her classroom. She learned rather quickly that if she was going to be successful as a classroom teacher, in an urban public school district in particular, she had better develop good classroom management skills immediately.

In her second year, this same teacher had a tremendous school year. Whenever she spoke to her students, you could hear a pin drop. When her students were engaged in cooperative learning, they were consistently on task. The achievement levels of her students soared, and many of them made the Honor Roll. What was the difference? Her classroom management skills improved tremendously. She committed herself to improving her classroom management so that her students could benefit from all she had to offer as a Language Arts teacher.

Attempting to teach a classroom full of students with poor classroom management skills is tantamount to stepping into a boxing ring to fight the heavyweight champion of the world with absolutely no boxing skills or experience in prize fighting. If you are going to enjoy success as a classroom teacher, you must also be successful as a classroom manager.

Creating a Classroom Environment that is Conducive to Learning

The classroom environment of African American children must be one that is conducive to learning and the attainment of academic excellence. I have witnessed on numerous occasions that when the classroom environment is conducive to learning, the probability for learning increases. On the other hand, when the classroom environment is conducive to failure, the probability for failure increases. It is therefore your responsibility to ensure that your students have the opportunity to learn in an optimal learning environment. Following, I will discuss several necessary components for creating a classroom environment that is conducive to learning.

A. Classroom Mission, Vision and Objectives

School districts and individual schools usually have their own mission, vision and objectives, but seldom do you find classrooms that have their own mission, vision and objectives. Towards creating an optimal classroom learning environment, it is good practice to develop a classroom mission, vision and objectives.

Mission

Your students need to know where it is that you want to take them as their teacher which helps them to develop a purpose for being in school in the first place. You should develop a mission statement which defines what your classroom is all about and what your students will accomplish as a result of being in your class. Your students can even participate in its development. Once the mission statement has been developed, it should be posted on the classroom wall in some visible location. The mission statement should be reviewed with your students regularly which again, reinforces what your classroom is all about. In creating a classroom environment that is conducive to learning, your mission statement conveys to your students that they are in your classroom for a specific purpose and that this is not the place for any distractions, disruptions or deviations to occur.

Vision

Consistent with your class mission is your class vision. Your class vision tells your students where you expect them to be over a period of time. This vision may go well beyond the year that they are with you as their teacher. Your vision is essentially a statement of what your students will achieve in the future as a result of their experiences as students in your classroom. As with your mission statement, your vision statement should also be written and posted on the wall in a visible location and reviewed with your students regularly.

Objectives

Now that you have determined a mission and vision for your students, what specific objectives do you have for your students relative to achievement for the current school year? Your objectives are statements of the specific outcomes you expect your students to achieve by the end of the school year. For example you may want to set academic objectives in terms of the number or percentage of students who will achieve the Honor Roll by the end of the school year or pass standardized tests. Or you may want to set attendance objectives in terms of your classroom average daily attendance percentage. You may even want to set classroom discipline objectives relative to reducing the number of rule infractions committed compared to the previous school year. Once your objectives have been determined, they should be written and posted along with your mission and vision on the wall in a visible location and reviewed regularly.

B. Wall of Fame

In Chapter Three - Motivating Your Students, I discussed the importance of recognizing and celebrating student achievement relative to inspiring your students towards achieving academic excellence. To that end, I indicated that it is good to create a "Wall of Fame" in your classroom for displaying all classroom achievement and attendance awards, and student work. In creating an environment that is conducive to learning, the displaying of classroom achievement and attendance awards, and student work reinforces for your students that their classroom is one where academic excellence is important, desired and expected. It reminds your students that the focus of their classroom is learning and achievement. Additionally, students feel good about themselves when they have the opportunity of having their accomplishments on display for their peers and parents to see. This in turn enhances the overall learning environment. In creating your classroom environment, be sure to always recognize student achievement by displaying achievement and attendance awards, and student work on your wall of fame.

C. Positive Message Signs

During my high school years, it became very difficult for me to stay focused on academics due to my strong interest in athletics. As a tactic of reminding me of what was most important, my mother wrote and posted short positive messages all over our apartment. Everywhere I went in the apartment, which included the bathroom, there were signs with short positive messages she had written. I recall laughing at these signs frequently, not realizing that they were shaping me subliminally. In hindsight, I am certain that my mother realized that there was power in these signs.

When I became a classroom teacher, one of the first things that I did was to create my own positive message signs and posted them all over the classroom. I didn't do this because I had consciously thought about what my mother had done. I did this because by this time, I understood the power in these messages. I understood that just seeing these messages on a regular basis was putting positive thoughts into the minds of my students. Although I was a new and young teacher at the time, I understood that my signs were enhancing the overall environment of my classroom. I also used the signs to have discussions with my students about the significance of the meaning of the messages and how they were relevant to their overall growth and development. By having my room filled with positive motivational messages, I was creating a classroom environment that was conducive to learning.

When I became an assistant principal, during my first week of school, I asked the principal if I could post my signs on the hallway walls and he obliged. The next morning before school began, I posted about one hundred signs of thirty different messages all over the building. Not only did the signs enhance the overall appearance of the building, but numerous students informed me that they were reading the signs regularly. My intentions were for these signs to be contributory towards creating a school-level environment that was conducive to learning.

As a principal, I have thus far worked in three different schools. In each school, I have posted my motivational signs all over the building. I posted them in the main office, the front lobby and every hallway. I even have signs posted in every classroom in the building. No matter where you go in my school, positive messages are absolutely unavoidable.

Currently, I am using eighty different quotes which include:

- No one can stop me from achieving greatness.
- The only person who can stop me is me.
- The price of success is total commitment.
- Education = Liberation.
- Education is the key to my success.
- Success comes only to those who work for it.
- I am striving to turn my dreams into reality.
- My destiny is greatness.
- I am a winner.
- Knowledge is Power.
- I will consistently make the Honor Roll.
- I will consistently make Student of the Month.

• I will achieve academic excellence.

As a classroom teacher, the overall environment of your classroom must be positive, motivating, stimulating and conducive to learning if optimal learning is going to occur. In your efforts of closing the achievement gap between African American and white students, a classroom environment that is conducive to learning is an absolute must. Filling your classroom with messages that are positive and motivating within the context of a society that is inundated with messages of negativity and despair is certainly a step in the right direction towards increasing the probability that your students will achieve academic excellence.

D. Positive Image Posters and Pictures

In addition to positive messages, African American children need to be bombarded with positive images. This begins with the pictures that you display in your classroom. I remind my teachers all of the time that their students are inundated with not only negative messages, but negative images as well. As the classroom teacher, you must counteract this negativity with as much positiveness as you can. This begins with the images that are on your classroom walls. African American children need exposure to images of positive African Americans who have done great things in history such as Mary McLeod Bethune, Fannie Lou Hamer and Anna Julia Cooper for girls, and Marcus Garvey, Malcolm X and Dr. Martin Luther King, Jr. for boys.

As a classroom teacher, in addition to my wall of fame and positive messages, I also reserved wall space for approximately twenty five different posters and pictures of positive African Americans or in other words; African American heroes and heroines. I also ensured that my students learned about all of the individuals on the posters.

In creating a classroom environment that is conducive to learning, I recommend that you obtain posters and pictures of people who are positive and serve as the types of role models that African American children need to look up to. Images of positive African Americans in your classroom send the message that you value their contributions to society and that they represent the types of models that you desire for your students to pattern themselves after. You must also be sure to create lessons that teach your students about the people you have showcased in your classroom.

E. Desk Arrangement

The arrangement of student desks is another area that lends itself to creating an environment that is conducive to learning. As with all of the components discussed towards creating an optimal learning environment, teachers must carefully plan how they are going to arrange their classrooms which include the arrangement of student desks.

The arrangement of student desks speaks to the teacher's approach to instruction. If the teacher utilizes a teacher-centered instructional model, chances are that the desks are set up in rows. If the teacher utilizes a student-centered instructional model, chances are that the desks are arranged in clusters. As student-centered instruction enables the teacher to engage the students in their own learning, it also gives the teacher the opportunity to make better use of the space in the classroom. In other words, when the desks are arranged in clusters, no one section of the classroom is the front of the room and no one section is the rear of the room. As the teacher circulates the room, all sections become the front because the teacher is literally all over the room. Since the desks are not arranged in rows, there's no problem of any students having to sit in the rear of the room.

The arrangement of student desks also speaks to the teacher's organization skill. When there is organization to the desks, the probability for effective classroom management increases. Conversely, when there is a lack of organization to the arrangement of the desks, the probability for effective classroom management decreases. Towards creating and sustaining a classroom environment that is conducive to learning, you must give a great deal of thought to how you will arrange your students' desks and have a good rationale as to why they are arranged as they are.

F. Bulletin Boards

Bulletin boards are another critical area towards creating a classroom environment that is conducive to learning. Your bulletin board layout should be well planned and thought out so that it is consistent with the overall focus of your classroom. For example, you may have a monthly theme where your bulletin board is reflective of the theme, or your bulletin board may reflect a particular unit you are covering in a particular subject area. As the classroom teacher, it is your responsibility to maintain your bulletin board while keeping it current and keeping it relevant. You should refrain from putting up bulletin boards that use commercial materials. Bulletin boards are much more meaningful when they are developed by the classroom teacher. Neatness and organization in your bulletin board layout is also imperative.

G. Chalkboards

In Chapter Five - Planning and Organization, I discussed the importance of preparing your chalkboard before the arrival of students relative to organization. It is equally important that your chalkboard is fully prepared before students enter the classroom relative to classroom management and creating a classroom environment that is conducive to learning. In teaching and managing your students, they require your full and undivided attention. Taking the time to write long passages on the chalkboard gives students the opportunity to lose focus. Your objective must be for your students to maintain their focus for the entire day.

Additionally, in creating an environment that is conducive to learning, your chalkboards are an integral part of your learning environment. They must always be reflective of the learning that is to take place in your classroom. In other words, there's nothing worse than for students to enter a classroom where the board is not reflective or instructive of what will occur on a given day. Blank chalkboards translate into a lack of preparation on the part of the teacher. They are also reflective of a classroom that is less than conducive to learning. Students should never have to enter a classroom where the learning environment is less than optimal.

H. Cleanliness

I can't overemphasize the importance of cleanliness in

your classroom relative to creating a learning environment that is conducive to learning. I have observed on numerous occasions that learning is less than optimal when students are subjected to not only an unorganized learning environment, but also an unclean learning environment. Students must be conditioned to keep their classroom clean at all times. You must encourage your students to pick up after themselves throughout the course of the day. If you are a subject area teacher, your students must be conditioned to pick up after themselves and straighten out their areas at the conclusion of each period. In creating an environment that is conducive to learning, the cleanliness of the classroom is an absolute must.

Classroom Management

If you are going to be effective as your students' teacher, you must be an extraordinary classroom manager. Classroom management proficiency is not something that happens by chance. Towards becoming an extraordinary classroom manager, you must effectively plan for classroom management success. As all facets of teaching require thorough planning, classroom management is no exception. The development of a classroom management plan is a critical component to your overall effectiveness as a classroom teacher.

In creating your classroom management plan, you must first ask yourself the question, "What are the things that I must do in order for my classroom to function in a manner that maximizes the probability for optimal student learning to occur?" You would then brainstorm everything that you would need to do in your classroom relative to effective classroom management. After you have brainstormed your list, you would proceed to develop a classroom management plan which details everything that you need to implement from the beginning of the school day up until dismissal. Following are key components for you to consider towards developing your classroom management plan.

A. Rules, Consequences and Rewards

In creating your classroom management plan, you must first establish a set of rules, consequences and rewards that serve as its foundation. Your rules, consequences and rewards provide your classroom with the structure that it will need in order to ultimately run itself.

Rules

In establishing your classroom rules, you should have no more than five. Anything over five becomes excessive. These five basic rules become the foundation for your behavioral expectations in your classroom. This doesn't mean that you don't have other behavioral expectations. It simply means that these five are your core expectations which drive all others.

There are no particular rules that would be considered the best rules or the most appropriate rules for managing your classroom. You may initially develop one set of rules but determine at some point later that there is a need to revise them. This determination might be made because of your own unique circumstances with the students you teach. When I taught, I had five basic rules which served as the core of my behavioral expectations. They were:

- Always treat one another with respect.
- No talking except when given permission or when appropriate. Raise your hand to be acknowledged.
- No walking around the room unless given permission.
- No food, candy or gum permitted in the classroom.
- Never litter and always pick up after yourselves.

Of course, I had other behavioral expectations, but again, these served as the core of my expectations for all the years that I taught.

Consequences

Once you have determined your classroom rules, you must then determine consequences for breaking your rules. Again, there are no particular consequences that would be considered the best or most appropriate for violating your rules. This is a decision that you will have to make. As with rules, you may find that your consequences need to be revised based upon your own unique circumstances. When I taught, my consequences were very simple. They were:

- first infraction - warning (name written on the board)
- second infraction - after school detention
- third infraction - call parent
- fourth infraction - visit parent

You'll notice that nowhere do I indicate administrative intervention. I never felt that the building administrators were going to be able to solve my behavioral problems for me. I knew that if I sent my students to the office, once they were returned to me, I would inevitably still have to deal with the problem. I therefore took the initiative to either call or visit the parents of my students. Once I visited a parent, I had no further problems with any students in my classroom.

Rewards

Rewards is an area where so many teachers fail. Developing a set of rewards makes student compliance with your rules so much easier. The implementation of a rewards system enables you to reinforce expected behaviors. So many children; particularly African American children residing in urban communities are subjected to so much criticism and negativity that they become almost immune to it. This is why even with the best rules and consequences, many teachers continue to experience difficulties with classroom management. When rewards are issued for exhibiting expected behavior, you increase the probability for the expected behavior to become permanent. Keep in mind, that it is not required that rewards are tangible. Rewards can simply be praise given for exhibiting expected behavior. In other words, when students engage in the behaviors that you expect of them which include being in compliance with your classroom rules, you need to verbally acknowledge the behavior and let them know that you appreciate their efforts in exhibiting appropriate behaviors.

Your rules, consequences and rewards should be written or typed on signs to be posted on your classroom wall. The letters should be large enough for all of your students to be able to see from wherever they sit in your classroom.

On the first day of school, you must spend a considerable amount of time introducing your rules, consequences and rewards to your students. They should also be required to write them in their notebooks or student planners so that they can be referred to whenever the need arises. It would also be good practice to send a copy home to your students' parents for them to read and sign as acknowledgement of having reviewed them with their children.

As you proceed into the week and school year, it is imperative that you review your rules with your students regularly; particularly at the start of each week or month, depending on your students' level of compliance. The key is consistency in enforcement of your rules. If you lack consistency in your enforcement of your rules, you are going to experience difficulty with the overall management of your classroom. If your rule says for example, that you must raise your hand to be called upon, you must enforce this rule consistently. If your consequence says that you will call parents, you must call them. When students see that you are lax in enforcing your rules, they tend to violate them. Your objective is to raise the achievement levels of African American students. If your classroom is not well managed, raising the achievement levels of your students becomes a virtual impossibility.

B. Students Entering Your Classroom

Whether you are a self-contained teacher or a subject area teacher, you must establish procedures for your students to enter your classroom at the start of the day and for each period of the day for subject area teachers. Your procedure for students entering your classroom sets the tone for the day or the period. If your students enter your classroom chaotically, chances are good that you are going to have a chaotic lesson. If your students get into a routine of entering your classroom orderly and focused, chances are good that you are going to have an orderly and focused lesson.

Entering Your Classroom at the Start of the Day

As students arrive to school in the morning, depending on the procedures of the administration, they either line up or have the opportunity to play. Ideally, they will be lined up outside before entering the building. Once the students are under your supervision, you must ensure that they are mentally ready to enter your classroom for learning before physically entering the room. Before your students enter your classroom, you should have them line up in one or two straight, orderly and quiet lines outside of your classroom door. At this time, be sure to formally greet them. You must then ensure that they have settled down and that they know exactly what you expect of them upon entering. For example, they may be required to go right to their lockers or coat closet and hang up their coats. They may then be required to sit down in their assigned seats and take out their books, notebooks, pens/pencils, and whatever materials they may need. They may then be required to work on the "do now" assignment on the board while you take attendance. Once all of the morning routines have been completed, you can proceed to your first lesson.

Entering Your Classroom at the Start of Each Period

Whether you are a subject area teacher or a self-contained teacher, you must prepare your students for entrance into your classroom before entering. Subject area teachers teach several different classes so this routine will take place throughout the day. Self-contained students only leave the room for specials and lunch.

As students arrive to your classroom, they must be conditioned by you to line up in one or two straight, orderly and quiet lines outside of your door in order to listen to your instructions. Proceed to greet them formally and then remind them of your expectations of what they should do upon entering your classroom. For example, you should require them to go to their assigned seats, take out their textbooks, notebooks, pens/pencils and other required materials and proceed to work on the "do now" while you take attendance.

From the start of the period, there should never be opportunities for your students to have nothing to do. Whenever your students are allowed to sit idly without productive work, they are essentially being given opportunities to engage in undesirable behaviors which can evolve into behaviors that are difficult to modify. It is your responsibility to ensure that your students are always engaged in meaningful and productive class work assignments.

Once your students have entered your classroom, either at the start of the day or at the start of a period, they should be conditioned to come into your classroom to work on some sort of a subject-related "do now." The "do now," which should take no more than five minutes will provide you with the opportunity to take attendance and perform whatever other tasks you may need to engage in before formally commencing your instruction. This way, you do not have to use valuable class time to take attendance while students sit in their seats doing nothing. During the taking of attendance, your students can remain busy. As students are working on your assigned "do now," behavior becomes less of an issue as all students are required to complete your assignment within the allotted five minute timeframe.

C. Students Exiting Your Classroom

At the conclusion of the period, students must be conditioned to clean up around their desks, straighten up their desks and to line up in a straight, orderly and quiet line. This way, your students are leaving your classroom in good condition and ready for the next class to arrive. By organizing your students at the end of the class, you are setting the tone for them for their next period class. You should also remind them of your expectation to walk quickly, quietly, orderly and on the right hand side of the hallway as they proceed to their next destination. They should always be encouraged to arrive to their next destination within your school's time allotment between periods.

If it is dismissal time, your students should engage in the same routine as mentioned above relative to straightening up the classroom so that minimal effort has to be made towards preparing the classroom for the next school day.

D. Circulating Your Classroom

Teaching students and sitting down are not compatible behaviors. I've observed on numerous occasions the attempt by teachers to sit down at their desks and teach their class. When this occurs, the teacher cannot see the entire class and many of the students cannot see the teacher. This translates into a recipe for chaos. Towards becoming an effective classroom manager, you must always be able to see what your students are doing and they must be able to see that you see what they are doing. Also, they must all be able to see you. Once your classroom management is where you want it to be, you will be able to be less visible.

As an effective classroom manager, you must circulate your classroom often as students are engaged in their work activities. In this way, no one part of your classroom is the front of the room because you are on your feet circulating the entire room. On the one hand, your circulating the classroom enables you to be visible for your students, but on the other hand, it enables you to monitor your students as they engage in cooperative learning activities.

Again, I cannot overemphasize the significance of being on your feet throughout the day. You cannot sit down, teach and be effective. You must be on your feet circulating your classroom (with the exception of teachers with physical disabilities).

E. Anticipating Problems

It is a given that it is inevitable that problems such as conflict between students will arise at some point during the year. The key is how effectively you deal with them. Will you respond to them effectively when they occur? Will you anticipate them happening and therefore be prepared to prevent them from escalating? Or will you be so unprepared for problems that when they arise, they destroy the fabric of your learning environment?

In your role as classroom manager, you must always anticipate the worst, but expect the very best. As soon as your students enter your classroom, your "antennas" must go up. You must become perceptive to all of the different attitudes and issues that your students will be bringing into your classroom daily. If you detect tension between students for example, you must be prepared to deal with it before it blossoms. If you do not deal with it immediately and effectively, at some point during the period or the day, this tension may escalate into a verbal or physical altercation in your classroom.

Towards anticipating problems, you must become quite familiar with your students. You must know who likes who and who dislikes who. You must be knowledgeable of the various interpersonal relationships amongst your students. You must also know your students beyond the academic side. When you truly know your students, you are in a much better position to anticipate and therefore respond to any potential problems that may occur in your classroom.

Effective classroom managers have their "antennas" up at all times. They know when there are problems and have a plan in place for handling whatever problems may arise. For example, when teachers' "antennas" are up, there is a good chance that they will detect when there is tension between students although the students haven't expressed any hostility towards one another. They can then be sure to keep the students separated until there is time to either talk to them, counsel them or send them to the guidance counselor for counseling or mediation. Ineffective classroom managers' "antennas" are down. If there is tension between students, they are probably oblivious to it. As the class proceeds, the tension mounts and the next thing these teachers know, they've got a fight to contend with.

If you are going to maximize student time on task, among other things, you must be able to anticipate all problems that may arise in your classroom. Again, anticipate the worst, but expect the very best.

F. "Transitions"

I have observed over the years that "transitions" can be quite challenging for not only the new teacher, but the veteran teacher as well. When I use the term "transition," I am referring specifically to the times when the teacher goes from teaching a lesson to some other activity, such as collecting work, or starting a new lesson after collecting work. A transition period could adversely impact behavior if you do not anticipate it or have a plan for managing it.

Typically, when changing from one activity to another, students tend to use this time as conversation time. If you can manage this effectively, the talking will not be much of an issue. If on the other hand you cannot manage the transition in general or the conversations in particular, you run the risk of losing valuable teaching time for the next lesson as you are now spending time trying to settle your students down from the transition. When reviewing your overall expectations with your students, you must be sure to address transitions and therefore condition your students towards making the transition from one activity to the next without engaging in conversations or other disruptive behaviors.

G. Leaving the Classroom During Instructional Time

At various points of the day, your students are going to want or need to leave the classroom for such things as to use the bathroom or to go to the nurse. The desire to leave your classroom has implications for your classroom management. If you have a revolving door of students leaving your classroom, it will be rare that you will have your entire class together at one time at any given point of a particular lesson or period. This will mean that the students leaving are going to miss something that was taught. The movement in and out of the classroom will also invariably cause distractions as students will want to see who is leaving or entering the classroom. You must therefore devise a plan for students leaving your classroom during instructional time.

Towards retaining as many students in your classroom as possible during instructional time, you must condition your students to the importance of your lessons. They must be made to understand that at no point can they afford to miss what you are teaching. Your students must understand that missing parts of your lesson could translate into failure or at least less than optimal performance on your assessments. There will be times however, that your students simply must use the bathroom. The times that you should emphasize use of the bathroom then are before the first period class or first lesson begins, and before or after lunch. Students should also be conditioned to ask permission to use the bathroom only for emergencies if it is during instructional time.

H. Assignment of Student Jobs

The key to good classroom management is a feeling of ownership of the classroom by your students. They need to feel that your classroom is also their classroom and therefore have a genuine concern for the overall functioning of the classroom. To that end, I strongly recommend that you give your students different classroom responsibilities. Although this is typically thought of as an elementary level strategy, it also works well at the middle school level. Of course, not all students will have opportunities to have jobs. That is not a problem however. The students that need to be targeted in particular are the students who are most prone to be disruptive or exhibitors of undesirable behaviors. These are the students that you'll want to focus upon. If you are successful towards getting them to feel a sense of ownership of your classroom, they will be less inclined to engage in inappropriate behaviors.

I. Arriving to Class Prepared

Each and every day, your students must arrive to your class not only prepared mentally, but also in possession of all the supplies and materials needed in order to be productive. You must encourage and condition your students to always bring to class their notebooks, textbooks, pens / pencils and whatever other supplies and materials you may require. When students arrive to class unprepared for learning, you run the risk of classroom management problems. Valuable time has to be wasted on discussing the importance of coming to school or class fully prepared and ensuring that the unprepared students are nevertheless accommodated for the day or period so that they can still be successful.

The best way to address students that come to class unprepared is to gauge it before teaching your lesson of the day. In other words, during your "do now," this is when you will need to determine who is unprepared and to make provisions for it so that again, valuable class time is not wasted.

J. Assigning Homework

Assigning homework is actually a "transition" but it deserves special attention. The assignment of homework can be a classroom management breakdown if you don't have a plan for handling it. In no way should you end a lesson and proceed to verbally give the homework assignment. When you do this, you run the risk of students not hearing or understanding all of what was said. This will require you to have to repeat the assignment and therefore waste valuable class time. All homework assignments should be written prominently on the chalkboard to enable all of your students to be able to read them and write them in their homework pads, student planners or notebooks. When it is time to give a homework assignment, your students should be conditioned to write the assignment while no one is talking. This way, they are concentrating on what is being written which eliminates the possibility for error. It also enables you to maintain control over your classroom.

As you develop your overall classroom management plan keep in mind that at the core of your plan are your rules, consequences and rewards. Whatever you decide will comprise your rules and consequences, be sure to be consistent and fair. Also, be sure to enforce your rules. Don't write one thing and do another. You will lose the respect of your students. Equally, regarding your consequences, don't write one thing and then let your students get away with a given infraction. And lastly, if your list of consequences say that detention will occur for example, don't have your student stand in the hallway instead. Whatever your consequences state will occur, make sure that this consequence does in fact occur.

7. MAKING CONNECTIONS

As a teacher of African American children, you have no choice but to be successful towards raising the achievement levels of your students. If you are not successful, your students will not be successful which will result in the perpetuation of African American underachievement in your classroom.

I have been saying over the years, that in order for teachers to experience success in the classroom, "connections" must be made with their students on a daily basis. Let's digress for a moment and engage in a short exercise. Hold your hands up in front of your body with your palms facing each other and fingers apart. Now bring your hands together so that your fingers interlock. Once they interlock, bend your fingers down so that both hands are clenching one another. Now grip both hands tightly so that if someone tried to pull them apart, it would be virtually impossible. If you have done this correctly, your grip is very tight. One could say that the hands are almost coming together as one. A solid connection between both hands has therefore been made.

This analogy represents what should be occurring in your classroom - solid connections. In other words, your instruction should result in students learning. As a result of your efforts towards preparing lessons that are consistently engaging, connections with your students should be an ongoing occurrence.

Now hold your hands up again. This time, instead of your fingers interlocking, attempt to move your hands together, but this time, have them miss one another as they are coming together without touching at all. The ending position should be that your arms are now up in the form of an "x" because no connection was made. As in algebra, we will say that the "x" represents the unknown, with the unknown being all that your students will never learn if meaningful connections are not being made in your classroom.

With achievement levels being what they are for African American children, this analogy represents what is actually happening in the lives of teachers and many of their African American students in classrooms across the country. In other words, the teachers and the students are missing each other which results in little learning taking place in comparison to white students because connections are not being made to the extent that significant improvement in achievement becomes the norm. If your students are not learning as a result of your instructional practices, African American underachievement will remain to be a national crisis.

Towards making meaningful connections with your students in the classroom, your pedagogical strength is only half the battle. In addition to being pedagogically strong, you must also be "people" strong. You must know your students beyond their academic side and be able to forge meaningful relationships with them. When you can relate to your students and your students can relate to you, the probability for their success in your classroom increases. Relating with your students then becomes critically important in order for learning to occur. As you learn to relate with your students, making connections in the classroom becomes less challenging. Following, I will discuss strategies for making connections with your students possible.

A Positive Attitude

Your attitude will determine in large part whether or not meaningful connections will be made in your classroom. As a teacher of African American students where again, the achievement gap between African American and white students continues to be alarmingly wide, it is crucial that you bring a positive attitude and a positive outlook to your students on a daily basis. The attitude you bring to your students will set the tone for them each day. If you bring a positive attitude to your students, you increase the chances that they will also be positive because the attitude that you bring to your students has a way of rubbing off onto them. If on the other hand you bring a negative attitude to your students, you increase the chances that they will also be negative. It is you who sets the tone for the overall climate of your classroom. Regardless of how you may feel mentally on any given day, you must ensure that your attitude is conducive to you making meaningful connections with your students each and every day.

Your attitude is conveyed to your students by the things you say, by the things you do and by the way you look. You must therefore ensure that you remain conscious of what impact your words and actions may have on your students.

A. What You Say

As the teacher of the classroom, you are also the leader of your students. A careful analysis of the challenges and obstacles associated with residing in urban communities will reveal that negativity is a pervasive reality of many of the students you teach. You therefore have a responsibility to offset this negativity with positiveness. In other words, while in the presence of your students, you must always be sure to speak positively to them. When your words are negative, you are contributing to the negativity that is already in so many of their lives. For example, when you see your students in the morning or at the start of a new period, be sure to always give your students a warm "hello." Giving your students a warm greeting before school begins or before the period begins enables you to start the day or period on a positive note. On the other hand, I have seen teachers who don't even bother to greet their students when they arrive to school or class. They give the impression that they don't want to be bothered with their students and that they wish they would simply go away. In these classes, you can rest assure that meaningful connections are not being made and consequently, optimal learning is not taking place.

B. What You Do

What you do is also important towards making connections with your students. Keep in mind that your students are watching every move that you make in their presence. Everything you do in the presence of your students should therefore be positive. For example, I strongly suggest that male teachers in particular get into the habit of greeting their male students with a handshake on a regular basis. This should be done while looking the students directly in the eyes. Greeting your students with a handshake while looking them in the eyes speaks volumes about yourself and how you feel about your students. It conveys the positive feelings that you have for your students and speaks to the positive attitude that you bring to your classroom.

C. How You Look

One of the worst things you can do in the presence of your students is to always look depressed, distressed or "evil." This does not mean that you must always wear a smile on your face while teaching. You can exhibit positiveness without wearing a smile, although there is nothing wrong with smiling as long as it doesn't adversely impact your classroom management. Your facial expressions should at least convey to your students that you do in fact want to be in their presence. Your facial expression is the outward expression of how you feel inside. It conveys to your students the attitude that you bring to your classroom. When your students perceive that you have a negative attitude and therefore do not desire to be in their presence, the chances for you making the kinds of connections that are necessary for learning to occur diminish drastically. You must therefore be cognizant of how you look relative to exhibiting a positive attitude towards your students in your classroom.

Treating Your Students With Respect

If you are going to be able to make meaningful connections with your students, you must be able to demonstrate a respect for your students. If you do not respect them, they in turn will not respect you with the end result being that optimal learning will not occur. A typical school year lasts for 180 days or more. This represents an enormous amount of time that you spend with your students. Within and throughout this time, trust between your students and yourself must be established and maintained. Children cannot learn from teachers that they do not trust. The trust that you must gain from your students must be earned. It does not come automatically. It is earned through how you treat and relate to your students. In other words, if you are going to be effective as your students' classroom teacher, you must treat them all with respect while simultaneously demonstrating care and concern for their overall development and well-being. Following are three critical areas that you should hone in on towards ensuring that mutual respect is the norm in your classroom.

A. Communicating With Your Students

When communicating with your students, you must always communicate with respect. Communicating with respect increases the probability of developing trust between your students and yourself which is essential towards building healthy teacher - student relationships.

When communicating with your students, you must refrain from any form of unnecessary yelling and screaming. Yelling and screaming are a turnoff for children and usually yield ineffective results. Over a period of time, students typically become immune to regular yelling and screaming by their teacher which incidentally has little if any effect towards achieving intended outcomes.

Being confrontational and argumentative with your students should also be avoided. Confrontations and arguments between yourself and your students are counterproductive towards making meaningful connections in your classroom. They engender unwanted and unneeded hostility in your learning environment. Always remember that when communication between you and your students becomes confrontational, the probability for learning decreases exponentially.

Whenever you communicate with your students, you should strive for positive communication as frequently as possible. Never engage in "put downs," condemnations and ongoing criticisms. As the classroom teacher, your job is to build your students up; not to tear them down. When your students do and say things which make you angry, as the professional educator in the classroom, you must always remain cognizant that they are children and will therefore make mistakes along the way which is an integral part of the maturation process of being a child. You must never allow their actions to anger you to the point that you engage in putting them down. Through positive interaction with your students, you must be able to explain to them why it is that you disagree with their actions and engage them in positive discussions about appropriate behavior. Again, whenever you communicate with your students, always do so with respect.

B. Treating Your Students Equally

More than likely, your students are very adept at discerning whether or not they are being treated equally. It is very easy to show favoritism towards those students that are your higher achievers to the expense of the students that are your lower achievers. Looked at another way, it is also easy to show favoritism towards those students that exhibit appropriate and desirable behaviors to the expense of the students who are disruptive. In treating your students with respect, it is imperative that you treat all of your students equally, which includes along racial and gender lines. When students sense that they are not being treated equally, it becomes easy for them to conclude that they are not respected. When students do not feel respected, less than optimal learning will occur which invariably translates into behavioral problems. As the classroom teacher, you must always treat your students equally. Each of your students must be able to sense that they are liked, appreciated and respected equally by you, their classroom teacher.

C. Treating Your Students Fairly

Not only do your students want to be treated with respect and equally, they also want to be treated fairly. You must always be mindful to be fair in your treatment of your students. When your students detect that they are not being treated fairly, you run the risk of lowering the morale of your entire class. For example, I have observed over the years that out of frustration due to disruptive behavior, the teacher will detain the entire class after school; despite the fact that the entire class was not disruptive. Consequently, those students who exhibited appropriate behaviors will in turn develop perceptions that their teacher is not fair towards disciplining students.

Another example I have seen before is denying an entire class an opportunity to attend a class field trip because of the actions of a percentage of the students in the class. Again, the perception of the well-behaved students is that the teacher is not administering fair disciplinary measures since all students are being penalized. As the classroom teacher, you must always strive to ensure that your treatment of your students is fair, equitable and respectful.

Respect for Your Students' Community

In addition to treating your students with respect, towards making meaningful connections with your students, you must also have the utmost respect for their community. It has been my firm contention for many years that the only teachers who should be teaching in urban schools, which are the schools where the overwhelming majority of African American children attend, are the teachers who genuinely want to be there. If you are there solely because you couldn't get a position in a suburban or rural school district or because the urban school district was paying more than the others, there is a good chance that you are doing your students a disservice because you had no real desire nor intention of teaching African American children in an urban environment. Instead, your employment is circumstantial at best.

Once you have nevertheless made the decision that you are going to accept the position and teach in this environment, you must ensure that you respect the students in your classroom and the community in which they reside because after all, the students that you teach are a product of their community environment. In other words, they *are* their community. Your students and their community are therefore inseparable. If you do not respect your students, you do not respect their community. If you do not respect their community, you do not respect them. When you do not respect your students' community, trust me - they will sense this through what you say and what you do.

Your objective is to make connections with your students in order to ensure that learning is taking place in your classroom. Your students must see you as being "down to earth" and not someone who sees himself being "above" them or their community.

Before moving on, I want to point out that in reading this section on respect for your students' community, one may get the impression that I am speaking specifically to non-African American teachers. This is not the case at all. I am speaking to all teachers of African American students. In other words, one can be African American and not have respect for the community of one's students. My contention is that regardless of the race or ethnicity of the teacher, respect for your students' community is of paramount importance.

A. Leaving School at Dismissal Time

There is a perception in urban schools, that when teachers leave school close to the time that the students are dismissed, that there is a fear of being in the community after school hours or close to dark. I have spoken with many students over the years who have this perception of the teachers they see zooming out of the parking lot before the students have even arrived home. Of course, some teachers have to leave early for a variety of reasons such as night classes, picking up or meeting their own children or second jobs. The problem however is the perception. As your students' teacher, it is important that your students do not have this perception of you. If your students perceive that you actually fear the community in which they live, they may also perceive that you do not respect the community in which they live either. This in turn will make it that much harder for you to make the necessary connections in your classroom in order for your students to become successful. I therefore recommend that on certain days of the week, if you are one who typically leaves school early, that you remain for at least an hour so that your students can see that you clearly feel at home in their community.

B. Negative Comments Made to Your Students

There's a fine line between highlighting negative aspects of your students' community for instructional purposes and putting the community down. If you are having a class discussion for example, on some of problems associated with urban communities, you must be sure that the comments you make are constructive for your students. If your students perceive that your comments are a condemnation of their community, you are going to drive a wedge between them and yourself. Once this wedge has been established, it will be difficult for you to successfully remove it because in the eyes of your students, you have criticized their community which in their world, is essentially all they know. You must therefore always be cognizant of your responsibility to demonstrate respect for your students' community both in your actions and your speech.

Respect for the Teaching Profession

In addition to the level of respect that you must have for your students and their community towards making connections with your students, you must also have respect for the teaching profession in general. Just as your students must respect you as a person, they must also respect you as a teacher. If you do not respect your profession as a teacher, it is going to be rather difficult for your students to respect you as their teacher.

It is my opinion that the teaching profession is the most noble profession of all professions. Everyone from all walks of life must pass through a teacher. You must remind your students of this frequently to enable them to appreciate the role of the classroom teacher.

Over the years, I have heard teachers complain to their students that teachers are not paid as well as professionals from other professions and that their students should therefore look to other professions when making decisions about their careers. I disagree with this vehemently. As a teacher, you must make your students aware of the fact that salaries should not and do not drive all career decisions; particularly with so many young promising teachers currently opting for careers other than teaching. You must encourage your students to view what you do as a teacher as important, significant and vital to the future of our society and our country. As your students gain an appreciation for the respect that you have for your profession, you increase the chances of them too having respect for the teaching profession. This in turn enables them to gain a greater respect for you in your role of teacher. As your students gain a greater respect for you in your role of teacher, making meaningful connections in your classroom becomes more and more possible. Always remember that if your students do not respect you, you will never be successful towards educating them.

Making Learning Fun, Stimulating and Engaging (revisited)

In Chapter Four - Effective Classroom Instruction, I made reference to the importance of teachers developing lessons that were fun, stimulating and engaging. This reference was made in the context of utilizing a student-centered instructional approach as opposed to teacher-centered instruction. Towards making connections with your students, the same rationale applies. You must be able to provide your students with instruction that is fun, stimulating and engaging. If your instructional practices enable you to inspire your students to enjoy learning, the probability for their academic success increases. If your instructional practices are boring and run the risk of putting your students to sleep, the probability for failure increases. Your lessons must therefore be well planned and thought out towards making learning interesting for your students. Despite the level of difficulty of your lessons and/or subject area, your task is to make learning as fun, stimulating and engaging as possible. When this occurs, students are more inclined to want to come to school everyday and take full advantage of all of the educational opportunities available to them.

Encouraging Critical Thinking

As you strive to make meaningful connections with your students by developing lessons that are fun, stimulating and engaging, you must always be mindful to encourage your students to become good thinkers. They must develop the ability to think for themselves. They must also develop the ability to think critically. You must therefore focus on asking questions that evoke critical thinking. If your questions dwell on lower-order thinking, your students will never develop into critical thinkers. You must concentrate on asking higher-order thinking questions which are both stimulating and thought-provoking. In other words, as a classroom teacher, you must be able to teach your students how to develop good critical thinking skills.

One of the best ways of teaching your students good critical thinking skills is to encourage your students to verbalize their thought processes which enables you to better understand how they think, how they process information and why they think as they do. This in turn will enable you to assist your students with the process of thinking a question or a problem through and reaching their own logical conclusions.

Familiarity With Your Students Beyond Academics

If you are going to make real connections with your students, knowing them beyond their academic side is unavoidable. If your focus is solely on the academic side of your students, you will miss the side that essentially drives the academic side - the social-emotional side.

If your school happens to be located in an urban community, you are teaching students who are products of an urban environment. Your students have therefore inherited the problems and issues that are associated with living in this environment. As the classroom teacher, you must be in tuned with the reality of living in an urban environment which includes how this reality impacts on your students academically, socially and emotionally. As you broaden your understanding of how the environment impacts on your students, you are in a much better position to fully understand your students as individuals.

When I was a classroom teacher, I understood the importance of really getting to know my students. I ate lunch with them in the cafeteria, I spent time with them after school and I visited their homes regularly. This way, I knew my students well. I not only knew my students academically, but I also knew them socially and emotionally. Towards closing the achievement gap, you too must strive to connect with your students by getting to know them beyond their classroom.

Referring back to the previous chapter on managing your classroom, invariably you will have students who are disruptive due to a lack of motivation which becomes evident during instructional time in your classroom. You will need to pay particular attention to these students if you are going to successfully educate all of your students. In other words, if they require all of your attention relative to discipline, you will have little quality time remaining for instruction. You must therefore have strategies in place which will increase your chances of keeping them focused which will in turn allow you to spend entire periods teaching.

A. Knowing Your Students' Interests

As you are striving to make connections with your students, you must strive to get to know your students. One way of getting to know your students is to learn their interests. Each of your students are unique and therefore have a variety of different interests. Your role is to learn those interests. Doing so not only increases the chances for you making connections with them, but it also provides you with relevant information towards keeping your students motivated and personalizing your instruction. For example, if you know that a student has a particular interest in business, you can craft your lessons in a way that engages him in instruction that is appropriate for the specific subject area, yet relevant to his unique interest in business.

B. Familiarizing Yourself With Your Students' Music

In my role of principal, I am known to encourage my teachers to listen to the music of their students regularly. These days, the music of choice is rap. Although there is some good in this art form, I find that the overwhelming majority of this music is quite negative and destructive, and therefore detrimental to the social, emotional and intellectual growth and development of its young African American listeners. The rap music that many of your students listen to frequently speaks to themes associated with violence, anger, drug glorification, sex and misogyny.

As a teacher of African American students where the overwhelming majority of the rap artists are also African American, you must be particularly mindful of the fact that many of these artists have become the role models of your students. This is so critically important to know because if your students are in fact receiving a steady diet of negative and destructive lyrics and in turn internalize the artists' messages while simultaneously identifying with what is being conveyed, the messages of the artists become the reality of your students. If these messages run counter to your efforts as the teacher, guess whose message has the most significance for your students. Again, you must familiarize yourself with your students' music so that you are better prepared to develop strategies to counteract these negative and destructive messages.

C. Listening to Your Students' Concerns

Another way of learning your students beyond the academic side is by genuinely listening to their concerns. Chances are that your students have a lot on their minds and that they are dealing with some very complex issues. If these issues are overwhelming for them, they are going to adversely impact learning. Although there are guidance counselors in the building, you are the one who spends the bulk of the day with your students. If you are successful towards developing solid relationships with your students and therefore making meaningful connections with them, chances are that they are going to share their thoughts and concerns with you. You must then be sure to take the time to listen to your students when they want to talk with you. This also helps to establish trust between your students and yourself.

Listening to your students' concerns gives you a wealth of information about them. It enables you to better understand your students; particularly when there are academic problems. You are then in a better position to address academic difficulties because you have a better understanding of the issues that are important to them and that they are therefore dealing with.

D. Eating Lunch With Your Students

A great way to make connections with your students is to eat lunch with them; particularly at the elementary school level. Eating lunch with your students from time to time enables you to spend an entire period discussing topics that are non-academic. As my students' teacher, I knew that a lot of my male students were interested in sports. I would therefore use some of the lunch periods to discuss sports with my male students and those female students who were interested in sports. These sessions were not confined to sports, however. We talked about a variety of topics which in turn enabled me to make solid connections with my students.

E. Making Home Visits

Making home visits is not for everyone, but they are an extremely powerful tool for those who make them. Going into your students' neighborhood and home environment provides you with a wealth of information about your students. When you visit your students in their homes, you get the opportunity to interact with them and their parents in their own environment without the distraction of the school itself and your students' peers. With your students being removed from the school environment, you get to know them on an entirely different level. Your students and their parents also get to see and interact with you on a different level as well. This in turn enables powerful connections to be made between yourself, your students and their families.

If you do decide to add making home visits to your repertoire of strategies, be sure to call the parents first to inform them that you will be making a visit.

F. Attendance at Student Functions

Many teachers miss golden opportunities here. It is one thing to attend functions that you as the classroom teacher organizes. It is something entirely different to attend functions that your students are participating in that you did not organize. When your students see you in the audience at functions that they know that you had nothing to do with organizing, it sends a message to them that they are important to you. This in turn increases the chances of you making meaningful connections with your students.

You Are a Teacher of Students - Not Subjects

Towards making connections with your students, you must always keep in mind that you are a teacher of students first; subjects second. Sometimes we tend to get this backwards. We spend so much time developing our knowledge of content and the other aspects of pedagogy that we forget that we must also have people skills. If we are going to be effective classroom teachers, we must be ever so mindful that it is the connections that we make with our students that will determine whether or not true success will become their reality. To that end, always be cognizant that as your students' teacher, you wear many different hats throughout the course of the school year which means that you function in many different roles. As an effective classroom teacher, you will simultaneously function in the roles of coach, motivator, counselor, mentor, role model, advisor, surrogate parent and friend. If you intend to make the kind of connections that will lead to your students' academic success, you must accept these roles with open arms and without reservation.

8.   HOLDING YOURSELF ACCOUNTABLE

As the classroom teacher, you are the number one determinant as to your students' academic success or failure. Your success as the classroom teacher translates into the academic achievement of your students. Conversely, your failure as the classroom teacher translates into the academic failure of your students. In your role of raising the achievement levels of African American students, it is unavoidable that you consistently hold yourself accountable for your students' academic success.

Refusal to Allow Student Failure

In your classroom, failure cannot be an option. You simply cannot allow failure to occur amongst the students you teach. As you have previously determined your purpose for teaching, and crafted your mission and vision for your students, you must now have a mindset that your students will be successful in your classroom. When teachers are of the mindset that they will allow failure to occur in their classrooms, failure will inevitably occur. When teachers are of the mindset that failure is not an option in their classroom, the probability for failure decreases dramatically. Why? Because the teachers have resolved that they will do all that is within their means to ensure academic excellence.

Developing a mindset where failure is not an option is by no means an easy endeavor. A study of the national achievement data by ethnicity will reveal the cold reality that African American children lag far behind their white counterparts in reading, writing, math and science. Upon taking on a teaching assignment at a typical urban middle school for example, chances are good that you would inherit a percentage of students who are working far below their potential and for a variety of societal reasons, are disinterested in what school has to offer. For a new or veteran teacher, the easy way out would be to simply blame the students, their parents and society for their students' academic deficiencies and lack of motivation to achieve and therefore not feel accountable for their students' achievement. In other words, since the achievement data indicates that African American children are performing at lower than desired achievement levels, it is easy and convenient for teachers to allow this pattern to persist in the classroom with the national achievement data serving as the justification. Teachers who hold themselves accountable for their students' achievement and who take the position that failure is not an option do not use current achievement data as justification for their students low academic achievement. For these teachers, failure is unacceptable and intolerable. These teachers therefore use the low achievement data as a source of motivation and inspiration. They want to prove to themselves, their students and anyone else who will listen that they can and will defeat the odds. In their classrooms, failure is not an option. They refuse to allow or accept failure to occur amongst their students.

In your efforts of ensuring that failure does not occur in your classroom, you must remind your students regularly that failure is not an option. You must in turn hold them accountable for high academic achievement, utilizing all of the strategies and principles discussed thus far. Additionally, it is imperative that your determination to ensure success comes from within yourself; not from external sources and pressures such as your administration. Your refusal to allow failure must be driven by your own internal belief that your students have the ability to achieve academic excellence. If on the other hand, your actions are driven by pressure from without, you will be less effective towards meeting your overall classroom objectives.

When I was a classroom teacher, one of the ways I motivated myself to refuse to allow failure to occur in my classroom was to hold myself accountable for my students academic achievement by taking personally any failure that may have occurred. In other words, if my students failed, I took the blame. Even if I knew in my heart that the cause of failure was beyond anything I could have done to effectuate change, I took their failure personally nevertheless. Why? Taking my students failure personally, forced me to "rise to the occasion." It forced me to "elevate my game." I was compelled to look within myself for strategies that worked or to search for alternatives to the strategies I was currently using. As long as I took the easy way out and blamed my students, their parents or society for their failure, I removed myself from being accountable. But once I looked at myself and held myself accountable for my students' success, I essentially made myself into a better teacher and educator as a result of my refusal to blame anyone other than myself for their failure.

In Chapter Two, I discussed self-reflection and self-assessment. I indicated that self-reflection and self-assessment must occur at the end of every school day. As a classroom teacher, whenever my students achieved grades on tests which were below the goals I had set for them, during my self-reflection, I thought long and hard about the preparation I provided and the test that was administered. During my self-assessment, as stated above, I took my students' failure personally. I pondered over what I could have done differently towards teaching the lessons and whether or not the assessment instrument truly measured what was taught. I literally convinced myself that it was something I either did or didn't do that resulted in my students receiving the grades that they received. I then planned the adjustments that were necessary for my students to be successful for the following day. In other words, as the classroom teacher, I refused to allow my students to fail. If they received failing grades, it was up to me to change what I was doing in order to increase the probability for success the following day.

Refusal to Make Excuses for Failure

Not only must you not allow failure to occur in your classroom, but equally important, you must not make excuses for any failure that may occur in your classroom. It is very easy to point the finger at others when your students are not performing at the level that you desire. But as I said in the previous section, as the classroom teacher, you must look within.

Over the years, I have listened to and even argued against the notion that the parents are the reason that so many African American children are not performing at proficiency levels. My position has always been that despite whatever problems that the parents may be experiencing, once the students are within the confines of the school, they are school personnel's responsibility. I remind any teacher that blames the parents that all who teach made a conscious decision that teaching is what they want to do with their lives. No one forced them to become teachers. Since they made a conscious decision to teach, it is their responsibility and obligation to become the very best teachers that they can possibly become.

It is your responsibility to effectively teach your students. You cannot be effective if you resort to conveniently blaming your students' parents, their community, the media or society for your students' academic shortcomings. Of course, as a professional educator, you should be aware that these variables all play a role towards shaping the thinking and attitude of your students. But by the same token, they cannot be used as excuses. Once you reach the conclusion that you cannot be effective because of external variables, you must also reach the conclusion that you are possibly in the wrong profession. If you are not successful in educating your students, your students simply will not be educated. Why? Because you are the number one determinant relative to the success or failure of your students. Within your repertoire of strategies for self-motivation, you must tell yourself regularly that nothing will stop you from making all of your students successful. You must never make excuses for any failure that may occur in your classroom. You must always hold yourself accountable for your students' success while maintaining the attitude that failure is not an option and excuses have no place in your overall practice of teaching.

Acceptance of Responsibility for Student Failure and Success

Once you have conditioned yourself to take responsibility for your students failure, you will become that much more effective as a classroom teacher. In other words, you will not allow failure, you will not accept failure and you will not make excuses for failure. In addition to accepting responsibility for failure in your classroom however, it is equally important that you accept responsibility for your students' successes. There is nothing wrong with accepting or taking credit for your students' success. You are the classroom teacher. If you are doing all of the things that you should be doing as a teacher, which includes the implementation of the strategies suggested in this book, chances are good that you are going to be an effective teacher. Towards becoming an effective teacher, which translates into your students experiencing success, you should feel quite pleased with yourself. You should in turn take full credit for the success that your students experience.

I recall as a 5th grade teacher, which was the graduation grade before entering middle school in the school I taught in, I would stand on the stage at graduation and literally boast about my students' achievement relative to report cards and standardized test scores. Each year, I was extremely proud of my students for their academic accomplishments. As I stood on stage boasting about their success, I knew that my students were successful because they had me as their teacher. I accepted full responsibility for their success. In my mind, they were successful because of what they experienced and what they were exposed to in my classroom.

Towards accepting responsibility for your students' successes and failures, it is imperative that you have and maintain high expectations for your students. If you do not expect for your students to do well, chances are good that they will not. Despite whatever circumstances that your students may be under, your expectations for your students' academic success must remain high. Once you have set expectations that are high, you must accept nothing less than academic excellence.

Again, you are the classroom teacher. When your students are successful, you must accept responsibility for their success. This becomes your motivation to continue to inspire your students to achieve academic excellence. Keep in mind that teaching is pretty much a thankless profession. Every so often, you will have parents to thank you for a job well done, but when your students are not doing well, the criticisms can be endless. The criticisms often outweigh the praise. This will require you to find means to keep yourself motivated. In the field of teaching, the best motivation is when your students achieve your goals. Acceptance of responsibility for your students success is the best motivation.

9. PROFESSIONAL DEVELOPMENT

As a classroom teacher of African American students where the achievement gap continues to be a persistent problem, it is most imperative that you stay abreast of all of the research on educating children in general and African American children in particular. What you learned in college may be completely obsolete within the first five years or less of your actual practice. You must therefore commit yourself to being a life long learner.

Life Long Learning

As a classroom teacher, you must be one hundred percent committed to reading. Your reading must be devoted to all aspects of strengthening your ability to improve the achievement levels of your students. Your reading should be comprised of the areas that I have covered in this book including the study of African and African American history, motivation, instructional practices and classroom management. You should also be committed to strengthening your knowledge of the content area(s) you teach to a level of expertise. No teacher should be in a classroom teaching children that is not an expert in their content area. This only further exacerbates the problem of low achievement amongst African American children.

Ongoing Participation in Professional Development

In addition to your reading, you must also commit yourself to attending professional development conferences, workshops and seminars. Participation in professional development activities not only allows you to learn from other professionals but it also gives you the opportunity to network with teachers from other schools and states.

In selecting sessions to attend, particular attention should be given to technology. Many teachers continue to struggle with the fast pace of technology. In some cases, teachers are actually intimidated by the computer. The computer is a wonderful classroom tool when the teacher understands its uses and applications. When participating in technology workshops with other novice users, the teacher can feel at ease that the other teachers in the room share similar frustrations.

Professional Organizations

Another way of staying current is to join professional organizations. Professional organizations provide a wealth of information on all aspects of education and they usually publish professional journals, books and newsletters. I strongly believe that all professional educators should be active members of professional organizations in order to remain current in the field of education and to be able to network with colleagues who are also members.

Developing a Collegial Relationship With Peers

In the field of education, it is imperative that teachers form collegial relationships with one another. In these times of sustained African American underachievement, teachers cannot afford to work and teach in isolation. Teachers must have a mindset of sharing. When a 7th grade teacher of math for example has strategies that work in her classroom with the result being that student achievement is high, but the students of the 7th grade math teacher next door are failing, those two teachers need to collaborate. The teacher of the low achieving students needs to be exposed to what the teacher of the high achieving students is doing. If they both work in isolation however, the high achieving students will be the only ones to benefit. Towards raising the achievement levels of African American students, all students must be exposed to teachers with best practices.

Ideally, your school's master schedule will provide for common planning or common prep periods to enable teachers to collaborate. During these periods, teachers can work, compare and plan together in order to increase the probability that all students have the opportunity to learn. The key here is that in closing the achievement gap between African American and white students, teacher collaboration must be the standard. If your school's master schedule does not permit for common planning or common prep periods, then teachers must make other arrangements to collaborate such as before school, during lunch periods or after school.

Willingness to be Observed by Colleagues

As an extension of developing a collegial relationship with peers, you must also be willing to allow your peers to observe your instruction and to provide you with constructive feedback. By the same token, you must also be willing to observe your peers so that you can learn from them. Again, collaboration cannot be underestimated. With the wealth of knowledge of all of the classroom teachers in a school, teachers must work together collaboratively in an effort to raise the achievement levels of all of the students in the school.

As a new, aspiring or veteran teacher of African American children, you must not underestimate the power of professional development and collegiality. Be sure to engage in sustained professional development through reading and attending professional development activities, and to maintain collegial relationships with peers.

10. A NOTE ON PARENTAL ENGAGEMENT

I started my teaching career back in 1988 as a long term substitute teacher of a 5th grade elementary school class in Brooklyn, NY. During that year, I learned very quickly that getting parents to be optimally involved in their children's education was going to be a real challenge. Meeting after meeting yielded very few parents in the audience. Of course, if students were performing, we had a very good turnout. Outside of student performances however, parent participation was disappointing at best.

When I did have the opportunity to interact with parents, I discovered quickly that many of them were looking for answers. They wanted to know exactly what it was that they could do at home to enhance their children's academic performance and improve their children's classroom behavior. As I provided them with answers and continued to work with them throughout the school year, over a period of time, I began to see noticeable differences in my students' academic performance and classroom behavior. As your students' teacher, you too must provide their parents with strategies they can utilize at home towards the enhancement of their children's academic performance and classroom behavior.

What's key however is developing a positive, productive relationship with your students' parents. On the first day of school or as close to the first day as possible, I strongly recommend that you contact your students' parents in an effort to introduce yourself and to share your expectations. You should also invite them into the school for a face-to-face visit. This shows them that you are genuinely concerned about their children's education.

Towards developing positive, productive relationships with your students' parents, you must ensure that you always treat them with the utmost respect; even the ones that are somewhat difficult. If you do not treat your students' parents with respect or your demeanor with them is condescending, you will never be able to develop the sort of relationship with them that your students require relative to increasing their chances for academic success. Your relationship with your students' parents will consequently be one of mistrust and a lack of respect. If you are going to be able to develop the kind of relationships with your students' parents that are positive and enable you to work together productively, you must strive to ensure that your relationships are built upon mutual trust and respect.

As a professional educator, you potentially have a great deal to offer to your students' parents. The reality is that while many parents possess a wealth of information and experiences towards working productively with their children, a large percentage of parents are struggling to keep their children focused and motivated. You must therefore be an asset to your students' parents who are struggling relative to offering and providing them with any information they may require towards strengthening their parenting skills. Doing so will increase the probability that your students will be successful in your classroom. Towards raising the achievement levels of your African American students, a relationship with your students' parents that is anything less than productive will inhibit the kind of progress that is desired. Be sure to always strive to build the types of relationships with your students' parents that will enable academic success to occur.

CONCLUSION

Throughout this book, I have offered strategies for teachers to utilize towards closing the achievement gap between African American and white students. If the strategies offered are implemented in earnest, there is no doubt in my mind that you and your students will experience success.

Over the years, I have seen time and time again that when the classroom teacher effectively implements strategies that work, the probability for student success increases significantly. On the other hand, when the classroom teacher fails to effectively implement strategies that work, the probability for student success decreases significantly. If African American students stand any chance for academic success, they must have teachers who possess the ability to make meaningful connections with them via utilizing strategies such as the ones offered in this book.

Towards being an effective teacher of African American students, I recommend that this book be read and studied regularly. I also recommend that all of the suggested books listed at the end of Chapter One be read as soon as possible if they have not been read already. Be sure to join as many professional organizations as you deem feasible and immerse yourself into the books and other professional materials that they offer. Finally, I strongly recommend that if you haven't read the book, *The First Days of School* by Harry and Rosemary Wong, that you obtain and read this book immediately. I consider this book to be a "must read" for all teachers towards ensuring that your students have the opportunity of achieving academic excellence.